CHICAGO PUBLIC LIBRARY
CONRAD SULZER REGIONAL LIBRARY
4455 N LINCOLN
CHICAGO, IL 60625

# SCIENCE, TECHNOLOGY, AND SOCIETY

# PIONEERS in SCIENCE

# SCIENCE, TECHNOLOGY, AND SOCIETY

## The People Behind the Science

KATHERINE CULLEN, PH.D.

Science, Technology, and Society: The People Behind the Science

Copyright © 2006 by Katherine Cullen, Ph.D.

All rights reserved. No part of this book may be reproduced or utilized in any form or by any means, electronic or mechanical, including photocopying, recording, or by any information storage or retrieval systems, without permission in writing from the publisher. For information contact:

Chelsea House
An imprint of Infobase Publishing
132 West 31st Street
New York NY 10001

**Library of Congress Cataloging-in-Publication Data**

Cullen, Katherine E.
  Science, Technology, and Society: the people behind the science/Katherine Cullen.
      p. cm.—(Pioneers in science)
  Includes bibliographical references and index.
  ISBN 0-8160-5468-1 (acid-free paper)
  1. Scientists—Biography—Juvenile literature. 2. Scientists—History—Juvenile literature. I. Title. II. Series.
  Q141.C76 2006
  509'.2'2—dc22                                        2004030605

Chelsea House books are available at special discounts when purchased in bulk quantities for businesses, associations, institutions, or sales promotions. Please call our Special Sales Department in New York at (212) 967-8800 or (800) 322-8755.

You can find Chelsea House on the World Wide Web at
http://www.chelseahouse.com

Text design by Mary Susan Ryan-Flynn
Cover design by Cathy Rincon
Illustrations by Bobbi McCutcheon

Printed in the United States of America

MP FOF 10 9 8 7 6 5 4 3 2 1

This book is printed on acid-free paper.

*I dedicate this book to
all future pioneers in science.*

# CONTENTS

| | |
|---|---|
| Preface | xi |
| Acknowledgments | xv |
| Introduction | xvii |

## CHAPTER 1
### Louis Pasteur (1822–1895): Cocredited for the Germ Theory of Disease and Developed First Vaccines — 1

| | |
|---|---|
| A French Education | 2 |
| Studies on Crystals | 3 |
| Fermentation | 6 |
| Only Life Begets Life | 7 |
| Savior of the Wine and Silk Industries | 9 |
| *Koch's Postulates* | *10* |
| The Germ Theory of Disease | 11 |
| Miracle Vaccines | 12 |
| Pasteur's Memory Honored | 15 |
| Chronology | 16 |
| Further Reading | 17 |

## CHAPTER 2
### Marie Curie (1867–1934): Discovery of the Elements Radium and Polonium — 19

| | |
|---|---|
| Polish Heritage | 20 |
| The Sorbonne | 21 |
| Two New Elements | 22 |
| A Doctorate and a Nobel Prize | 25 |
| Tragedy and Scandal | 26 |

|  |  |
|---|---|
| War Efforts | 27 |
| *The Nobel Prize in Chemistry 1935* | *28* |
| Death from Cancer | 29 |
| Chronology | 30 |
| Further Reading | 32 |

## CHAPTER 3
## Guglielmo Marconi (1874–1937): The First Transatlantic Radio Transmission — 33

|  |  |
|---|---|
| An Early Interest in Physics | 34 |
| Invention of the Wireless Telegraph | 36 |
| *Electromagnetic Waves* | *36* |
| Demonstration of the Utility of Wireless Telegraphy | 40 |
| Successful Transatlantic Transmission | 41 |
| The Father of Radio | 45 |
| Chronology | 46 |
| Further Reading | 47 |

## CHAPTER 4
## Sir Frederick G. Banting (1891–1941): Discoverer of Insulin — 49

|  |  |
|---|---|
| Farm Boy Becomes Military Surgeon | 50 |
| Repairing Childhood Deformities | 51 |
| Hormone X | 52 |
| A Miracle Cure | 57 |
| *Biotechnological Insulin Production* | *58* |
| Mistaken Credit | 60 |
| Silicosis and Wartime Research | 62 |
| Chronology | 64 |
| Further Reading | 65 |

## CHAPTER 5
## J. Robert Oppenheimer (1904–1967): Construction of the First Nuclear Weapon — 67

|  |  |
|---|---|
| Born with a Silver Spoon | 68 |
| Master of the New Physics | 69 |
| Theoretical Physics in the United States | 70 |
| The Controversial Manhattan Project | 71 |

| | |
|---|---|
| *Enrico Fermi* | 74 |
| A Question of Loyalties | 79 |
| Chronology | 81 |
| Further Reading | 82 |

## CHAPTER 6
## Rachel Carson (1907–1964): The Dangers of Pesticide Overuse — 85

| | |
|---|---|
| An Emerging Author | 86 |
| Studies of Life | 87 |
| Merger of Two Loves: Science and Writing | 88 |
| Greater Success | 89 |
| Threat of a Silent Spring | 91 |
| Negative Reaction—Positive Change | 95 |
| *The Environmental Protection Agency* | *96* |
| Pioneer of the Environmental and Ecological Movements | 96 |
| Chronology | 98 |
| Further Reading | 99 |

## CHAPTER 7
## William Shockley (1910–1989): Inventor of the Transistor — 101

| | |
|---|---|
| Specialization in Solid-State Physics | 102 |
| The Old Technology | 102 |
| Semiconductors | 104 |
| *The Team* | *104* |
| The First Transistor | 106 |
| Controversy | 109 |
| Initiation of the Computer Revolution | 110 |
| Chronology | 112 |
| Further Reading | 112 |

## CHAPTER 8
## Patrick C. Steptoe (1913–1988): Pioneer of In Vitro Fertilization — 115

| | |
|---|---|
| A Royal Navy Volunteer | 116 |
| Development of Laparoscopic Surgery | 117 |
| A Complementary Partnership | 118 |

| | |
|---|---|
| Initial Promising Results | 120 |
| Perseverance through Failures | 121 |
| Success! | 123 |
| *Modern ART* | *124* |
| Hope for Millions | 125 |
| Chronology | 126 |
| Further Reading | 127 |

## CHAPTER 9

### Kary B. Mullis (1944– ): Invention of the Polymerase Chain Reaction — 129

| | |
|---|---|
| An Explosive Introduction to Chemistry | 130 |
| A Winding Road to an Interesting Molecule | 131 |
| The Concentration Problem | 132 |
| Beauty in Simplicity | 135 |
| Gradual Acknowledgment | 137 |
| *A Stable Enzyme* | *138* |
| Positive and Negative Publicity | 140 |
| Chronology | 141 |
| Further Reading | 142 |

## CHAPTER 10

### Ian Wilmut (1944– ): The First Cloned Mammal — 143

| | |
|---|---|
| The Development of an Interest in Development | 144 |
| The Unplanned Path to Dolly | 146 |
| A Frenzied Response | 150 |
| *Reproductive v. Therapeutic Cloning in Humans* | *150* |
| After Dolly | 152 |
| Many Hopes | 153 |
| Chronology | 154 |
| Further Reading | 156 |

| | |
|---|---|
| Glossary | 157 |
| Further Resources | 163 |
| Index | 169 |

# PREFACE

Being first in line earns a devoted fan the best seat in the stadium. The first runner to break the ribbon spanning the finish line receives a gold medal. The firstborn child inherits the royal throne. Certain advantages or privileges often accompany being the first, but sometimes the price paid is considerable. Neil Armstrong, the first man to walk on the Moon, began flying lessons at age 16, toiled at numerous jobs to pay tuition, studied diligently to earn his bachelor's degree in aerospace engineering, flew 78 combat missions in Korea as a brave navy pilot, worked as a civilian test pilot for seven years, then as an astronaut for NASA for another seven years, and made several dangerous trips into space before the historic *Apollo 11* mission. He endured rigorous physical and mental preparation, underwent years of training, and risked his life to courageously step foot where no man had ever walked before. Armstrong was a pioneer of space exploration; he opened up the way for others to follow. Not all pioneering activities may be as perilous as space exploration. But like the ardent fan, a pioneer in science must be dedicated; like the competitive runner, she must be committed; and like being born to royalty, sometimes providence plays a role.

Science encompasses all knowledge based on general truths or observed facts. More narrowly defined, science refers to a branch of knowledge that specifically deals with the natural world and its laws. Philosophically described, science is an endeavor, a search for truth, a way of knowing, or a means of discovering. Scientists gain information through employing a procedure called the scientific method. The scientific method requires one to state the problem and formulate a testable hypothesis or educated guess to describe a phenomenon or explain an observation, test the hypothesis experimentally or by collecting data from observations, and draw conclusions from the results. Data can eliminate a hypothesis, but never confirm it with absolute certainty; scientists may accept a hypothesis as true when sufficient supporting evidence has been obtained. The process sounds entirely straightforward, but sometimes advancements in science do not follow such a logical approach. Because humans make the observations, generate the hypothesis, carry out the experiments, and draw the conclusions, students of science must recognize the personal dimension of science.

Pioneers in Science is a set of volumes that profile the people behind the science, individuals who initiated new lines of thought or research. They risked possible failure and often faced opposition but persisted to pave new pathways of scientific exploration. Their backgrounds vary tremendously; some never graduated from secondary school, while others earned multiple advanced degrees. Familial affluence allowed some to pursue research unhindered by financial concerns, but others were so poor they suffered from malnutrition or became homeless. Personalities ranged from exuberant to somber and gentle to stubborn, but they all sacrificed, giving their time, insight, and commitment because they believed in the pursuit of knowledge. The desire to understand kept them going when they faced difficulties, and their contributions moved science forward.

The set consists of eight separate volumes: *Biology; Chemistry; Earth Science; Marine Science; Physics; Science, Technology, and Society; Space and Astronomy;* and *Weather and Climate.* Each book contains 10 biographical sketches of pioneering individuals in a subject, including information about their childhood, how they entered into their scientific careers, their research, and enough background science information for the reader to appreciate their discoveries and contributions. Though all the profiled individuals are certainly distinguished, their inclusion is not intended to imply that they are the greatest scientists of all time. Rather, the profiled individuals were selected to reflect a variety of subdisciplines in each field, different histories, alternative approaches to science, and diverse characters.

Each chapter includes a chronology and a list of specific references about the individual and his work. Each book also includes an introduction to the field of science to which its pioneers contributed, line illustrations, photographs, a glossary of scientific terms related to the research described in the text, and a listing of further resources for information about the general subject matter.

The goal of this set is to provide, at an appropriate level, factual information about pioneering scientists. The authors hope that readers will be inspired to achieve greatness themselves, to feel connected to the people behind science, and to believe that they may have a positive and enduring impact on society.

# ACKNOWLEDGMENTS

I would like to thank Frank K. Darmstadt, Executive Editor of science and mathematics at Infobase Publishing, for his skillful guidance and extreme patience, and to Melissa Cullen-DuPont, for having all the answers. Appreciation is also extended to illustrator Bobbi McCutcheon for her dedicated professionalism and to Ann E. Hicks for her constructive suggestions. The reference librarians and support staff of the main branch of the Medina County District Library, located in Medina, Ohio, deserve acknowledgment for their assistance in obtaining interlibrary loans, acquiring numerous special requests, and handling the hundreds of materials and resources the author borrowed during the writing of this set. Gratitude is also expressed to Pam Shirk, former media specialist at A. I. Root Middle School in Medina, Ohio, for sharing her expertise. Many people and organizations generously gave permission to use their photographs. Their names are acknowledged underneath the donated images. Thank you all.

# INTRODUCTION

Science, technology, and society (STS) is among the fastest-growing *interdisciplinary* subjects taught on college campuses today. As a field, STS emphasizes science and technology as major forces that affect change at all levels of society, from the individual to the entire global arena. STS is concerned with the interactions among science, technology, and society. The relationship between science and technology is mutualistic; both depend on one another to continue growing and expanding. Science seeks to understand how the world functions; technology exploits the newfound scientific knowledge that, in turn, can lead to more fascinating discoveries. For example, science elucidates the process of DNA replication, and technology develops recombinant DNA cloning. The new technology allows molecular biologists to explore the function of a specific protein, perhaps an enzyme involved in the repair of genetic mutations. Understanding how the new protein works might lead to the development of a genetically engineered bacteria strain that turns out to be particularly useful for exploring the effects of carcinogens. Scientists perform basic research in order to gain new information that kindles technology to develop new procedures or new machines. The innovative technology then allows for even deeper probing to gain fresh insight. The processes complement each other. Though commercial profit often is the motivation behind the development of new technology, the true scientist at heart delights in the excitement of being the first to do/find/learn/make something. Society determines what improvements current technology needs, what important questions require answering, and what projects are worthy of financial support from the government. The opinions and feelings of society's members dictate rules (legal, moral, and ethical) on the permitted uses of new technologies ranging from the generation of nuclear power to genetic engineering and the development of high-tech satellite surveillance to biological sex change operations.

To illustrate the breadth of the field of STS, consider the many levels of society that science and technology may affect within a single subject, health awareness. At the individual level, a pregnant woman declines the offer of a new prenatal test due to her personal perception of the risks it poses to her fetus and herself compared with the benefits of knowing the test results. A community explores the dangers associated with living near a biohazardous waste facility. Nationwide, family care physicians worry about the decreased amount of daily physical activity of schoolchildren due to the popularization of video games. Globally, a hole in the ozone layer that normally filters ultraviolet radiation from the Earth's atmosphere leaves human beings at greater risk for sunburn and skin cancers.

Though everyone certainly can benefit from knowledge related to STS, people employed by the media particularly benefit, since they are the ones responsible for conveying information about new scientific discoveries or technological breakthroughs to the general public. An STS specialist might work for a biotechnology company as a consultant advising on the best way to market a new genetic test or as a salesperson explaining to medical personnel how the test works. The military utilizes people knowledgeable in STS for their weapons development programs, to assess the risks of new weapons, weigh these risks against the possible benefits, and make recommendations about what course to pursue. A sociologist might research the effects of electronic mail on how communities operate or on the social interactions between individuals. Expertise in STS helps economists to predict the impact of technological advances in information technology on the cost of national security.

Whether one views technology as a bane or a blessing, technological advancements guarantee that life will be forever changed. New discoveries constantly alter the way people live and give rise to entire new industries. When considering scientists whose contributions have had a tremendous impact on society, work performed by the following 10 individuals has transformed the way people think, work, play, and live. Louis Pasteur was a French chemist who figured out that microorganisms cause disease and pioneered the production and use of the first vaccines, saving countless lives. The Polish-born French physicist Marie Curie discovered the unstable elements radium and polonium and determined that the phenomenon of radioactivity was associated with individual atoms rather than their chemical interactions with other atoms. Her research led to new treatments for cancer and new sources of energy in addition to the eventual development of nuclear weapons. The Italian inventor Guglielmo Marconi transformed the field of communication by transmitting signals through the air using radio waves, becoming the first to send wireless telegraphic signals across the Atlantic Ocean. Sir Frederick Banting made one of the most important medical breakthroughs of the 20th century, the discovery of the hormone insulin and its use as a treatment for diabetes, a finding that still impacts more than 177 million people worldwide (in countries that report to the International Diabetes Federation) diagnosed with this serious illness.

Other scientific breakthroughs are more controversial, such as the development of the first atomic weapons. Directed by the American physicist J. Robert Oppenheimer, this technological accomplishment has affected global politics and economics in addition to the scientific fields that laid the foundations that made it possible. While science sometimes progresses faster than society can prepare to deal with the accompanying ethical issues, other times science brings attention to previously overlooked hazards. The American biologist Rachel Carson brought national attention to the dangers of pesticide overuse when she wrote *Silent Spring*, ushering in the environmental and ecological movements. The invention of the transistor by the American physicist William Shockley and others launched the computer revolution. Millions of infertile couples gained hope through obstetrician Patrick Steptoe's development of in vitro fertilization. The invention by Kary Mullis of the polymerase chain reaction paved new pathways in a variety of fields ranging from forensic science and genetic engineering to ecology and paleobiology. When Ian Wilmut cloned the first mammal from an adult sheep cell, he accomplished what scientists believed was only possible in science fiction.

That is what pioneers do—achieve the unimaginable by persisting through obstacles that others view as insurmountable. Advances in science and technology have promised much to society, but tomorrow's pioneers, those individuals willing to accept challenges, will surely deliver on those promises, as the pioneers mentioned above have. The scientists profiled in this volume of the Pioneers in Science set forged breakthroughs that led to the development of new technologies and transformed the lives of ordinary people. Their fields of expertise range from medicine to solid-state physics and from electromagnetics to developmental biology, but all have applied scientific principles to advance technology. This is not simply a book about inventors, but a story of pioneering scientists whose contributions have tremendously affected society.

# Louis Pasteur

(1822–1895)

Louis Pasteur's discoveries revolutionized health care, modern hygienic practices, and food production methods. *(AKG/Photo Researchers, Inc.)*

## Cocredited for the Germ Theory of Disease and Developed First Vaccines

Louis Pasteur was an imaginative scientist of the 19th century. The effects of his research profoundly affected society then and now. His research resulting in the process of *pasteurization* not only rejuvenated the French wine industry, but the process is still used today to reduce possible contamination and to extend the shelf life of many beverages. Pasteur was the first to figure out that microorganisms cause infectious diseases in animals and humans. He went even further by researching means of controlling the spread of harmful microorganisms and developed the first *vaccines* for many diseases, including rabies, anthrax, and fowl cholera. Modern hygienic practices stem from findings and recommendations from Pasteur's research. Because of his expansive work revealing the many relationships that humans have with microorganisms, he is considered a founder of *microbiology*, but interestingly, he began his scientific career as a chemist. In today's world, where numerous soaps, sanitizers, and household cleaners are plastered with the word "antibacterial" in order to move them off the shelves, it is difficult to imagine what life must have been like before Pasteur's contributions.

## A French Education

Louis Pasteur was born December 27, 1822, in Dôle, France, a small town near the Swiss border. His father, Jean-Joseph, had served as a French soldier for Napoleon I and at the time of Louis's birth was a tanner who made leather goods from animal skins. He was a quiet man filled with pride for his country and a great appreciation for learning. His mother, Jeanne, was the daughter of a gardener. Jean-Joseph had a big dream for his only son to become a teacher someday. Louis began his education at age six in the local school at Arbois, where his family then lived. He was an average student who liked to fish with his friends in a nearby river and had an artistic talent for drawing portraits.

By age 15, the headmaster at Louis's school recognized something special in him and recommended that his family begin to prepare him for testing to enter the École Normale Supérieure, a college for professors of arts and sciences. As a tanner, his father did not have much money, yet he wanted to give Louis the best preparation possible to help him to realize his dreams. He sent Louis to a boarding school in Paris to prepare for his future education. Louis, however, was not prepared for life in a big city and six weeks later returned home to Arbois, where he continued to excel at the local school. In 1839 Louis entered another school only 25 miles (40 km) away, Royal College of Besançon. He did well but still liked art and spent much time drawing portraits of friends and townsfolk. He earned a bachelor of letters degree in 1840 and started working on a bachelor of science degree. He was given a job as an assistant teacher to offset expenses. Two years later he passed his bachelor of science exam, and a few days afterward he took the entrance exam to the École Normale Supérieure. He ranked 15th out of the 22 students who were accepted, but this was not good enough for Louis, who turned down the offer of acceptance! Instead, he spent another year preparing by taking classes and giving lessons at a prep school, Lycée Saint-Louis. The following year he placed fourth on the entrance exam, and in 1843 he began his official training to become a professor.

## Studies on Crystals

At the École Normale Supérieure Pasteur studied mostly physics and chemistry. He especially enjoyed attending lectures given by a renowned chemist named Jean-Baptiste Dumas. This energetic chemist inspired Pasteur, whose passion for chemistry and science grew. He completed his doctor of science degree in chemistry in 1847, and his teachers strongly recommended him for a professorship, but Pasteur preferred to be in a laboratory doing research. So he accepted a position as a laboratory assistant for Antoine-Jérôme Balard, the man who discovered bromine (used widely today to purify pool and spa water).

While working on a doctorate degree, Pasteur's artistic nature attracted him to the beauty of *crystals*. Many substances such as table salt and sugar form unique crystals with sharp faces, regular angles, and beautiful colors. The structure of each crystal is dependent upon the arrangement of the *atoms* making up the substance. When light is shone through solutions containing some dissolved crystals, the light beam is bent. These crystals are called optically active. Sometimes the path of the light is bent to the right and sometimes to the left. Pasteur wondered why. Perhaps partially because his hometown Arbois was surrounded by vineyards, Pasteur decided to concentrate on crystals that naturally formed in wine vats, tartaric acid and racemic acid crystals. It was known that tartaric acid and racemic acid were made of the same components and even in the same proportions, yet tartartic acid crystals rotated light, and racemic acid crystals did not.

Pasteur spent much time in the lab examining crystals with a magnifying glass, sketching his observations, making his own special equipment to measure the way crystals bent light, and pondering this apparent puzzle. Then one day he had an epiphany. Because of his acute attention to detail and his remarkable intuition, he noticed that the facets, or flat faces, in tartaric acid crystals all pointed in the same direction, but in racemic acid they pointed in both directions. He made an educated guess that the facets pointing in two different directions somehow canceled each other out such that it appeared that the light was not bent at all. (This would be similar to adding a positive one and a negative one to a number—the end result makes it appear as if nothing was done.) Pasteur tested this hypothesis by painstakingly separating crystals with facets pointing in different directions using a microscope, making separate solutions of each, and measuring the light beam passed through each. His diligence was rewarded when he demonstrated that the light was bent to the right by one of the solutions and to the left by the other solution. News spread throughout the world of this young scientist's discovery. He had shown that the physical properties of *molecules* were dependent not only upon their composition, but also on their structures. At age 25, Louis Pasteur had founded a new branch of chemistry called *stereochemistry*, which is concerned with the position and arrangement of atoms in molecules and how their arrangement affects molecules' properties.

Shortly after this major discovery, Pasteur's mother died. He returned home briefly and then went to Dijon, where he worked as a physics professor. In January of 1849, he was appointed professor of chemistry at the University of Strasbourg. There he met Marie Laurent, the 22-year-old daughter of the university's principal. Within weeks he asked her father for her hand in marriage. They were wed in May 1849. Rumor has it that Pasteur worked the morning of his wedding day, and he had to be reminded to go to the church! Marie was an ideal mate for Louis. She seemed to understand his passion for science and supported him by handling home matters, assisting him in his writing, and forcing him to explain his

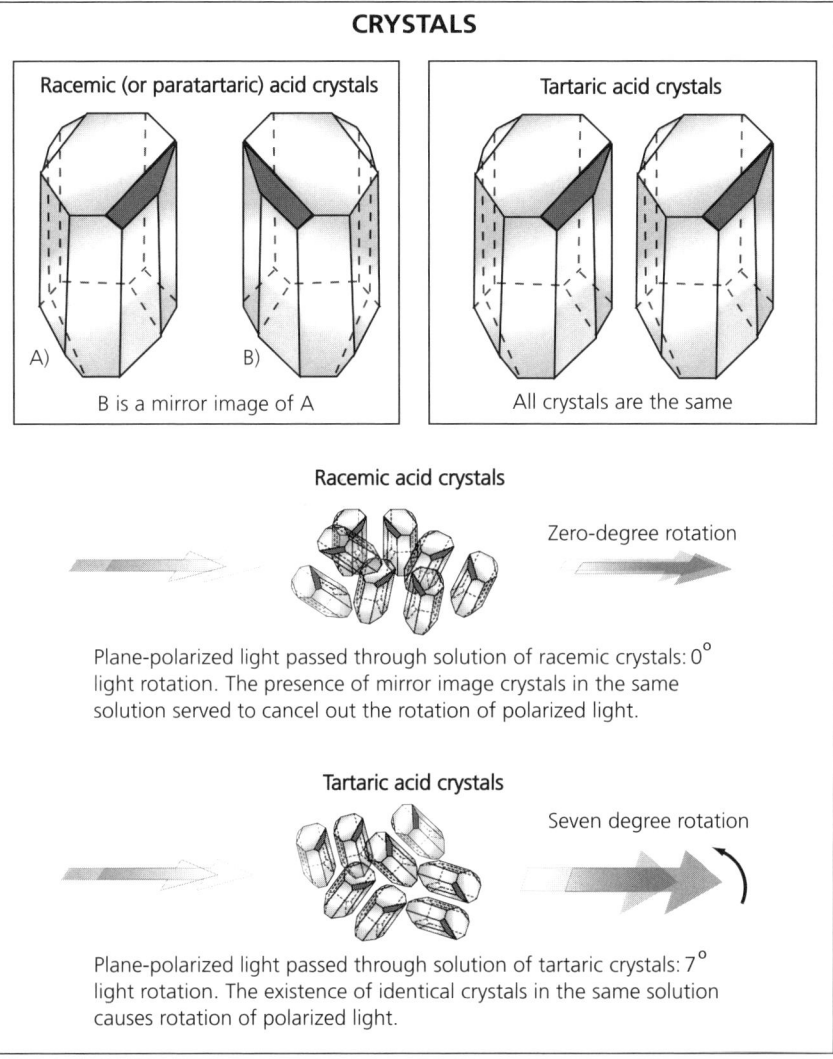

Pasteur noticed that the facets in tartaric acid crystals all pointed in the same direction, but in racemic acid they pointed in both directions.

research clearly. They had five children together, but sadly, only two survived into adulthood. Back then people did not know how to prevent or treat infectious diseases. Ironically, had his children been born into the next generation, which benefited from the knowledge of Pasteur's later discoveries, they might have all survived.

# 6 Science, Technology, and Society

## Fermentation

Pasteur took a new job as a professor of chemistry and dean of sciences at the University of Lille in 1854. He was still only 31 years old, not typical of a dean currently, and not typical then. At this point in his life, his work began to center on the applications of science to benefit society. The father of one of Pasteur's students owned a local factory that produced alcohol from beet juice. Unfortunately, the product sometimes spoiled, costing the industry money. The factory owner's name was Monsieur Bigo, and he turned to Pasteur for advice on this problem.

*Fermentation* is a process responsible for converting sugar into alcohol and carbon dioxide gas. At the time, it was thought that this was simply a chemical process, though people knew that yeast played some sort of role. Pasteur studied drops of liquids from the vats of Bigo's fermenting beets under the microscope and noted the presence of yeast but also of many other tiny objects in the souring vats. He proposed that these other objects were the basis of the problem. He suspected that fermentation was a biological process, that the yeast were living beings, and that they converted the sugar into alcohol by their normal metabolic processes. From these studies, Pasteur developed his famous germ theory of fermentation, which stated that microorganisms were the cause of fermentation and that specific types of microorganisms were associated with specific types of fermentation. While the yeast were making alcohol in the healthy vats, other contaminating microbes were producing undesirable substances in the souring vats. In this case, *bacteria* had overrun the yeast and were producing lactic acid (the same substance that sours milk). Other scientists laughed at this strange idea . . . yeast ate sugar, peed alcohol, and passed gas as a byproduct, but this mocking only fueled Pasteur's motivation. He did not like to be publicly ridiculed, and through the rigors of his experimentation, he gathered much supporting evidence for his hypothesis.

Pasteur was spellbound by these miniature creatures. He concocted special soups to grow them in his lab, where he could study their metabolism further. By placing tiny drops of liquid containing these organisms into a sterile flask of soup, within a day the new flask would contain millions of these dancing, swarming microbes.

Louis Pasteur  **7**

The remainder of Pasteur's scientific career revolved around the activities of these microscopic life forms.

## Only Life Begets Life

In 1859, Pasteur was named the director of scientific studies at the École Normale, where he himself had been a student. While the title was large, his workspace and funding were limited. He did his research in an attic lab with homemade equipment and incubated his microorganisms in a cupboard under a staircase. Nevertheless, during the next few years he took on one of his most famous challenges and moved from the study of chemistry further into the field of biology to unravel the origins of microbial life. At the time, many people believed that living organisms could arise spontaneously from nonliving matter. He had learned to grow microorganisms in a broth that

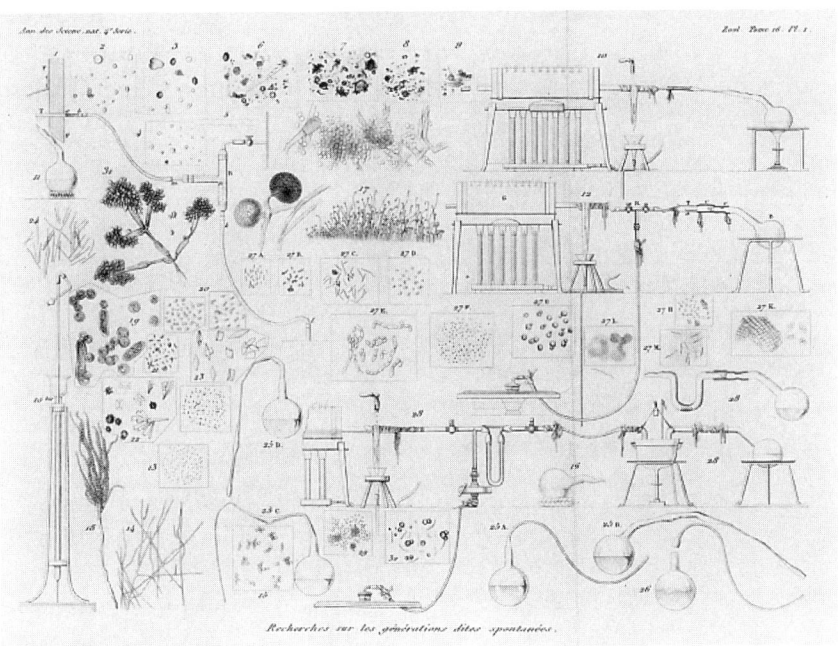

Spontaneous generation experiment. Pasteur showed that microbes responsible for decay and fermentation are from the air and do not arise spontaneously from the decaying matter. *(Library of Congress, Prints and Photographs Division [LC-USZ62-95258])*

contained sugars and salts necessary to support life. If bottles or flasks containing this broth, or culture media, were uncapped briefly and then resealed, after a few days the broth would be teeming with tiny organisms. Pasteur believed that the tiny life forms were carried in the air by dust particles that floated into the opened flasks. He hypothesized that cleaner air would have less microbes.

To test this hypothesis he exposed 20 flasks to air from the Arbois countryside. He carried 20 others by mule to a mountain peak and exposed them to the icy mountain air from the top of Mont Blanc. All the flasks were resealed and brought back to the lab where growth was allowed to occur. Eight of the countryside flasks became cloudy, but only one of the mountain air flasks did. Many people remained skeptical of Pasteur's claims. Some argued that there must be a life-giving component to air, rather than life floating around in the air itself. They thought that heating the flasks destroyed the ability of the air in a sealed flask to support life. This provoked Pasteur, who, by using swan-necked flasks, further demonstrated that the microorganisms arose from reproduction of preexisting microorganisms rather than spontaneously in the culture media. The unique shape of these flasks allowed air (including any magical life-giving components) to enter, yet would trap any dust particles and prevent them from entering the region of the flask that contained the broth. He boiled the liquid inside the flasks to kill any microbes that may already be present and then left them open to incubate. These flasks remained clear; no microbial growth occurred. When he tipped them to allow the sterile broth to contact the bend in the flask, growth soon appeared. This famous experiment put an end to the debates regarding spontaneous generation. Amazingly, some of these original flasks have been saved, and they remain clear more than 100 years later.

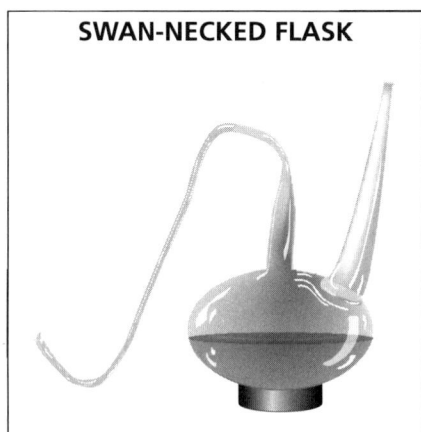

Pasteur used specially designed swan-necked flasks to disprove the theory of spontaneous generation.

## Savior of the Wine and Silk Industries

Meanwhile, Pasteur continued his studies pertaining to fermentation. He also taught about the chemistry of paints and about the relationship between health, comfort, and architecture at the École des Beaux-Arts in Paris. At this time, the emperor Napoleon III pleaded for Pasteur's help solving France's winemaking problems. France was famous for its wines, but sometimes they would become bitter or sour. Pasteur immediately suspected the cause of the problem was due to the presence of undesirable microorganisms in the fermentation mixture, as in beet juice. He set up a research lab in an old street café to examine this and found that most spoilage could be traced to a particular organism. In fact, he boasted that he could predict the problem for certain wines by examining the microorganisms present. This tickled the wine-tasting experts, who challenged him. Even though they tried to fool him by including perfectly good wines, Pasteur was able to distinguish successfully which wines were fine, bitter, or sour without even tasting them! He figured out that by treating the wine at 131°F (55°C) for several minutes, the harmful bacteria would be killed, but the taste of the wine would not be affected. Wine partially sterilized in this manner could be stored indefinitely. The process is now called pasteurization and with slight modifications is also used for vinegar, beer, juice, milk, cheese, and eggs. Thus Pasteur was not only able to determine the cause of the problem, he also developed a practical application utilizing the results of his research to assist the industry.

It is a good thing for France that Louis Pasteur's father had instilled such a love and devotion for his country into his only son. After saving the wine industry, the French government asked Pasteur to help the silkworm industry. Diseases of the silkworms, whose cocoons were used to manufacture fine silk, were ruining the French clothing industry. During the years of 1865–69, Pasteur spent every summer in Alais studying diseases of silkworms, including pébrine, which caused small black spots to appear on their skin. Microscopic analysis of these worms revealed small oval shapes—microbes. Pasteur predicted that pébrine could be controlled by picking out and destroying moths that showed signs of disease. However, when this was done, the newly hatched worms showed signs of a different disease that resulted in flabby bodies. Though he must have been discouraged not only by this but also by the death of his father and two of his daughters during this time, Pasteur persisted and was finally able to show that specific microbes caused specific diseases. As a lover of public demonstrations, he took batches of silkworm eggs, predicted which diseases, if any, the larvae would have, and was correct. Again Pasteur's impact was in the methods of application of his new discoveries.

He returned in the fall of each year to the École Normale, where now he was not only teaching but also in charge of student residential life. Being so disciplined himself, he was very strict, and the students complained, causing him to be relieved of this position. The school did not want to lose such a famous scientist, however, and gave him a new job as director of a lab. He was also made a professor at the Sorbonne at this time. Unfortunately, a stroke in 1868 left him partially paralyzed. Though he regained partial use of his legs and speech, he required assistance in carrying out his research from

## Koch's Postulates

The research of Louis Pasteur closely paralleled that of his rival, the German physician Robert Koch (December 11, 1843–May 27, 1910). Koch is considered a pioneer in bacteriology for identifying the anthrax and tuberculosis bacilli, developing staining techniques for identifying bacteria, and his investigations of cholera. Pasteur also researched anthrax and cholera, and he developed successful vaccines for both in addition to a vaccine for rabies. Koch developed a vaccine for tuberculosis, but to his embarrassment, it failed. Koch was awarded the Nobel Prize in physiology or medicine in 1905 for his investigations and discoveries in relation to tuberculosis, but unfortunately, Pasteur passed away before the Nobel Foundation was even established. Koch's name is memorial-

this point on. Also, the war between France and Prussia forced him to leave Paris temporarily. France was eventually defeated, which crushed Pasteur. He gave back an honorary doctorate degree that a German university had given him and turned down a job offer by an Italian university. Instead, he chose to do something that would help his mother country compete with Germany; he decided to study beer making. The problems France was having making beer mirrored the fermentation problems Pasteur had solved in beet juice and wine, and he was soon able to boost the economic success of the beer industry as well.

## The Germ Theory of Disease

Around 1877, Pasteur shifted his focus to the cause of disease. Perhaps this interest was fueled by the loss of so many loved ones. We are used to the idea that germs cause disease, but at the time this was a novel concept. Many believed that "bad air" or even human

---

ized in modern microbiology textbooks for proposing a series of tests designed to judge whether a particular organism caused a disease. These are referred to as Koch's postulates.

The first postulate states that the specific organism should be shown to be present in all cases of animals suffering from a specific disease but should not be found in healthy animals. The second postulate affirms that the specific microorganism should be isolated from the diseased host and grown in pure culture in the laboratory. The third criterion requires that when organisms from the pure culture are inoculated into a healthy laboratory animal, it duplicates the disease seen in the original animal. Finally, the same microorganism must be recovered from the artificially infected host. These measures are not faultless, since some agents of disease are difficult to grow in an artificial environment in the laboratory. In addition, in the case of human diseases, one cannot experimentally infect a host to qualify the third postulate. Nevertheless, Koch's postulates are a valuable set of criteria for determining whether a particular agent is the cause of a disease.

sinful nature was the cause of disease, ridiculous though this may sound in an age of hand sanitizers and antibiotics. Over the next decade, Pasteur was devoted to this and linked specific microbes to half a dozen human and animal diseases. Both he and Robert Koch are credited for the germ theory of disease, which states that diseases are caused by specific microbes. Pasteur went even further by suggesting that the spread of disease could be prevented by killing the microorganisms that caused them. In fact, it was Pasteur who recommended that carcasses of animals that died from anthrax be burned rather than buried. He is also credited for revealing the underlying principles that led to aseptic technique—keeping a sterile environment—during surgeries. At the time, entering a hospital was practically a death sentence. The surgeon who first used carbolic acid as an antiseptic during surgery, Dr. Joseph Lister, publicly expressed his gratitude to Pasteur for his contributions to the medical field and for the many lives saved due to his recommendations. (Lister's name is the root of the trademark for a popular antiseptic mouthwash.) After implementing aseptic techniques, deaths following operations dropped from 50 percent to 3 percent.

## Miracle Vaccines

Pasteur began by studying chicken cholera, which had killed one-tenth of all the chickens in France. He figured out how to grow the causative organism in the lab and then injected it into healthy chickens, which promptly became ill. Once, perhaps by accident, his lab assistant Émile Roux left some cholera cultures in the lab for an extended period of time while Pasteur and his assistants took summer holiday. Maybe nobody in the lab felt like doing the dishes before they left! When these old cultures were injected into chickens, the chickens become slightly ill, but surprisingly recovered. When these same chickens were later inoculated with fresh culture, they remained healthy! Pasteur recognized that what happened with these chickens paralleled what happened when Dr. Edward Jenner injected persons with cowpox as a means to prevent possible future infection with smallpox. These chickens had been "vaccinated" against cholera. Somehow the old culture had become weakened and lost its ability to cause fatal disease but prevented the chickens from catching this same illness in the future. Today scientists know this is because the immune system creates antibodies when exposed to specific microorganisms, and these antibodies remain in the system, preventing someone from becoming ill if they encounter those same microorganisms again.

By 1881, Pasteur had developed an anthrax vaccine using similar techniques. Anthrax was killing hoards of cattle and other grazing farm animals. During a huge public demonstration of this vaccine's usefulness in Pouilly-le-Fort, Pasteur's assistants inoculated 24 sheep, six cows, and one goat with his vaccine against anthrax. After 12 days, they inoculated these animals again. Two weeks after the second vaccine injection, he injected all those animals as well as 24 unvaccinated sheep, four unvaccinated cows, and one unvaccinated goat with fresh anthrax culture. Pasteur went home, probably worried what this incredible experiment would do to his scientific reputation if the result did not turn out as anticipated. He returned two days later to an already cheering crowd filled with not only farmers, but also with veterinarians, scientists, reporters, and officials who had come to witness the historic event. All the vaccinated animals were healthy, but 21 of the unvaccinated sheep and the one unvaccinated goat were already dead. The four unvaccinated cows showed signs of fever and swelling, and eventually the other three sheep and the cows died. Even the people who had laughed at Pasteur and criticized his cockiness a month before could not deny the overwhelming life-saving success of this new vaccine.

Next he turned to rabies. As a boy, Pasteur had witnessed the horrible effects of this disease. He had stood nearby and listened to screams of agony as victims of bites from mad dogs had their flesh wounds burned by the local blacksmith's irons in hopes of preventing the deadly illness. Rabies symptoms do not appear until a month or so after the *virus* is transmitted to a bite victim through the saliva of an infected animal, but by then there is little hope for recovery. The virus travels to the spinal cord and then throughout the body, causing paralysis and intense muscular spasms upon swallowing liquids. Death usually results from destruction of the portion of the brain that controls breathing. Today people are vaccinated only after being bitten by a rabid animal. This is possible because the incubation time is so long.

Because rabies is caused by a tiny virus, Pasteur was not able to find it using a microscope, nor was he able to culture the microorganism in the laboratory using the conditions he had perfected for many types of bacteria. But he didn't give up; instead he grew the virus inside living animals. Pasteur removed spinal cords from infected animals and dried them for varying lengths of time. He gave a series of successive shots containing these ground-up spinal cords to 50 healthy dogs. Each shot contained tissue that had been dried for less time than the previous shot; thus each shot was stronger than the last one. Finally, he gave shots to the animals that were of a strength that should have caused the disease itself, but none of the animals became ill or died.

On July 6, 1885, a desperate mother brought her nine-year-old boy to Pasteur. Joseph Meister had been bitten by a rabid dog more than a dozen times two days before. While Pasteur was confident in the success of his rabies vaccines in dogs, this was a human boy, and being a father himself, he was very concerned with whether he should attempt to vaccinate the boy. After consulting two physicians who both stated that the boy would most certainly die if nothing were done, Pasteur agreed to attempt the vaccine. As he could not bear to perform the act himself, he had an assistant give Joseph the series of 13 shots, sent the boy home, and waited, and waited, and waited. But the boy never became ill. It was a success!

Three months later, a 15-year-old shepherd named Jean-Baptiste Jupille was brought to Pasteur with pleas for the vaccine. This brave young man saved several younger shepherds by wrestling with and killing a mad dog that had come to attack them and their sheep. He was badly bitten. But it had been six days since the attack. Was it too late for the vaccine to work? It was not, and over the next few years, thousands more came to Pasteur for his miracle rabies vaccine. Despite the obvious success, some of his colleagues still claimed the vaccine was useless and even dangerous. They questioned how it was known whether the bite victims would ever have contracted the disease and worried the vaccine itself could cause rabies rather than prevent it. The English Commission on Rabies studied the issue extensively and, in 1887, declared that Pasteur's vaccine had indeed saved many lives.

## Pasteur's Memory Honored

The money that rolled in due to success from the rabies vaccine was used to set up a nonprofit biomedical research institute that specialized in the treatment of rabies and other microbiological problems. In 1888, the Pasteur Institute opened in Paris. In 1887, Pasteur had suffered two more strokes, and his health and memory deteriorated from that point on. While he was unable to perform much more research, Pasteur served as director of the institute until his death on September 28, 1895. A large public funeral was held in his honor at the palace in Versailles, and he was buried at the Pasteur Institute. Joseph Meister, who had received the first rabies vaccine, was serving as gatekeeper of the institute 45 years later during World War II when the Germans overtook Paris. He reportedly committed suicide rather than open up the tomb of the man who saved his life for the German soldiers.

Pasteur's legacy persists today and has expanded globally to more than 100 research units and 2,700 employees. Eight Nobel laureates have been employed by the Pasteur Institute. Its scientists have been responsible for many breakthroughs in biomedical research, including isolation of the AIDS virus, the development of numerous vaccines and sulfa drugs, the regulation of viruses, and cancer detection and treatment.

Louis Pasteur thrived on challenges. Though he was a quiet child, he was by no means a shy scientist. He was immensely confident in his own abilities and enjoyed proving his opponents wrong. Because of this, other scientists might have felt animosity toward him; however, the impact and applications of the results from his scientific studies were apparent to all. Any scientist would relish the notability brought about by any one of his individual studies, which have only been briefly outlined here. Pasteur was brilliant and had a knack for making logical and insightful predictions regarding his experiments and for knowing which lines of research to pursue vigorously. He did not limit himself to physics and chemistry, the fields in which he was formally trained, but instead considered himself simply a scientist. He felt that knowing how to form and test hypotheses from observations and previous data was more important than knowing all the content information in a given field. While he knew he could always look up specifics regarding his current topic of examination, he was an awesome experimentalist with a keen sense of intuition and a drive matched by few. Because of this, he became a legend during his own lifetime.

# CHRONOLOGY

| | |
|---|---|
| 1822 | Louis Pasteur is born on December 27 in Dôle, France |
| 1839–42 | Attends Royal College of Bensançon |
| 1842–43 | Attends the Lycée Saint-Louis in Paris |
| 1843–48 | Studies chemistry at the École Normale in Paris |
| 1844 | Begins chemical and crystallographic studies |
| 1845 | Receives a master of science degree |
| 1847 | Completes a doctor of science degree in chemistry |
| 1848 | Discovers role of facets on crystals |
| 1849–54 | Teaches chemistry at the University of Strasbourg |
| 1854–57 | Is dean of sciences at the University of Lille |
| 1856 | Begins to study fermentation in beets |
| 1857 | Introduces the germ theory of fermentation |
| 1857–67 | Serves as director of scientific studies at the École Normale |
| 1863–67 | Teaches science at the École des Beaux-Arts in Paris |
| 1864 | Gives spontaneous generation lecture at the Sorbonne and invents the process of pasteurization, which saved the wine industry |
| 1865–69 | Studies silkworm diseases in Alais |
| 1867–74 | Teaches chemistry at the Sorbonne in Paris |
| 1867–88 | Serves as director of the chemistry lab at the École Normale |
| 1871 | Begins beer fermentation studies |

| | |
|---|---|
| 1877 | Starts studying anthrax |
| 1880 | Develops chicken cholera vaccine and starts studying rabies |
| 1881 | Publicly demonstrates anthrax vaccine at Pouilly-le-Fort |
| 1885 | Joseph Meister receives first rabies vaccine; Jean-Baptiste Jupille receives second rabies vaccine |
| 1887 | The English Commission on Rabies issues its favorable report on the rabies vaccine |
| 1888 | Pasteur Institute holds opening ceremony |
| 1888–95 | Serves as director of the Pasteur Institute |
| 1895 | Dies at Villeneuve l'Étang on September 28 at the age of 72 |

## FURTHER READING

Allaby, Michael, and Derek Gjertsen, eds. *Makers of Science.* Vol. 2. New York: Oxford University Press, 2002. Chronological biographies of influential scientists. Includes political and social settings as well as scientific achievements.

De Kruif, Paul. *Microbe Hunters.* San Diego, Calif.: Harcourt Brace Jovanovich, 1954. Intended for adult readers, but does a wonderful job describing Pasteur and several other famous pioneers in the field of microbiology.

Dubos, René. *Pasteur and Modern Science.* Madison, Wis.: Science Tech Publishers, 1988. Written for adult readers, but superbly demonstrates the uniqueness of Pasteur's science and describes his experiments in detail.

Jacob, François. "The Pasteur Institute." Nobelprize.org. Available online. URL: http://www.nobelprize.org/medicine/articles/jacob. Last modified on June 29, 2004. Briefly summarizes Pasteur's life and work. Also discusses the history and accomplishments of his legacy.

Parker, Steve. *Louis Pasteur and Germs.* New York: Chelsea House Publishers, 1995. Intended for younger readers. Includes glossary and many illustrations and photos.

*Scientists and Inventors.* New York: Macmillan Library Reference, 1998. Brief profiles of the lives and works of more than 100 notable scientists. Written for juvenile readers.

# Marie Curie

(1867–1934)

Marie Curie discovered the chemical elements radium and polonium and pioneered the study of radioactivity. (© *The Nobel Foundation*)

## Discovery of the Elements Radium and Polonium

*Radioactivity*. The word conjures up mystifying images of fluorescent substances and research scientists wearing white coats, scarier images of decontamination teams and nuclear waste, and for some, a miracle cancer cure. In scientific terms, radioactivity is simply the emission of *subatomic particles* or energy from unstable nuclei. Some elements such as uranium, thorium, *polonium*, and *radium* are naturally radioactive for unknown reasons. Ever since the serendipitous discovery of radioactivity by the French physicist Henri Becquerel in 1896, physicists have been fascinated by its nature, and physicians have attempted to exploit its potential for destroying diseased cells. In order to appease both the scientists and the clinicians, elements that had such properties first had to be identified and isolated.

Madame Marie Curie was an extraordinary researcher who dedicated her life to unraveling the mysteries of radioactivity after discovering the radioactive elements polonium and radium. Her discoveries allowed scientists to reach a new understanding about the structure of atoms and opened a new field in medical treatment. However, unlike some scientists whose claims to fame are derived from a lucky breakthrough or from being at the right place at the right time, Madame Curie achieved international recognition for brilliantly recognizing the significance of her discoveries and for her years of exhausting dedication that ultimately caused her demise.

## Polish Heritage

On November 7, 1867, Marya Skłodowska was born near Warsaw, Poland. She was the youngest of five children whose parents were both trained educators. Despite the fact that Russia ruled Poland and was doing its best to eliminate all traces of Polish culture, the Skłodowskas secretly taught their children all they could about their heritage. These lessons gave Marya a great sense of her own identity and the confidence she needed to accomplish so much later in life.

In 1873, Marya's father was fired from his physics teaching position for not adhering to the strict Russian curriculum. To ease financial burdens, the family took in boarders, forcing Marya out of her bedroom and into the living room. Her mother suffered from tuberculosis, and the children were not allowed to kiss her. When Marya was eight, her oldest sister died, and when Marya was 10, her mother died. Marya was depressed, but despite these difficult circumstances she excelled in school and graduated at the top of her high school class at 15 years old. She learned to read French, German, and Russian in addition to Polish. Her goal was to become a science teacher like her father.

## The Sorbonne

Women could not attend universities in Poland, so Marya joined a Flying University to quench her thirst for knowledge. Flying Universities were revolutionary organizations that held clandestine meetings during which Polish patriots taught each other subjects such as mathematics, history, and science. Both Marya and her sister Bronia craved a real university education, and the Sorbonne seemed the perfect environment. France represented liberty to the two young girls who were raised under the oppressive czarist rule of Russia. Because money was scarce, they made a deal with each other. Marya worked as a governess to put Bronia through school, and then Bronia supported Marya so she could obtain her degree. While in Paris earning her medical degree, Bronia met and married an exiled Polish doctor. As promised, when she completed her own studies, she sent for Marya.

Marya was almost 24 when she moved to Paris in 1891. She registered at the Sorbonne under the French version of her name, Marie. At first she lived with her sister, but when Bronia's household became too distracting and the two-hour trip each way to school stole too much time away from her studies, Marie rented the first in what would become a series of cold, damp, attic apartments. Though her spoken French was satisfactory for conversation with other Polish students, Marie struggled to understand her science professors. Being a foreigner and one of very few females in her subject, she was an outcast and therefore had plenty of time to study. She lived on a frugal diet, walked everywhere since transportation was too expensive, and studied each night at the library, where the temperature was much more bearable. She became physically frail. Nevertheless, within 18 months, she not only earned her physics degree, but also was first in her class. One year later, she received a second degree in mathematics and was second among the candidates. This sort of determination was characteristic of Marie.

While she planned to return eventually to Poland to care for her father, she received a small grant to study magnetism. A friend from the university recommended she seek assistance from a 35-year-old teacher at the Paris Municipal School for Industrial Physics and Chemistry. His name was Pierre Curie, and he was respected in his field for research on magnetism and for discovering piezoelectricity (electricity generated when certain crystals are mechanically stressed). With his brother Jacques, he had also invented an electrometer for measuring small amounts of electricity.

Pierre and Marie found they shared an enthusiasm for learning, a passion for science, and love for each other. They were married in 1895 and went on a bicycle tour in Brittany for their honeymoon. Pierre and Marie worked long hours together in his lab investigating different aspects of magnetism. Pierre earned a doctorate degree in physics, and Marie obtained her teacher's diploma. They were able to share their dreams and their research as well as their lives. Their first daughter, Irène, was born in September 1897.

## Two New Elements

During this time, Marie was deciding on a topic for her doctoral dissertation in physics. No woman in Europe had ever earned a doctorate before, but Marie seemed not to take notice of that. In 1895, the German physicist Wilhelm Röntgen was researching *cathode* rays when he discovered a mysterious form of radiation that could pass through glass, wood, and even human flesh. He named them *X-rays* and then returned to researching other subjects. The following year, the French physicist Henri Becquerel hypothesized that X-rays were associated with *luminescence* (the emission of light). To test this, he put a luminescent material, potassium uranyl sulfate, on top of some photographic plates that were wrapped in thick layers of black cloth and exposed them to sunlight. When the plates were developed, they had darkened spots on them, indicating that the substance emitted some form of radiation that passed through the black cloth to expose the plate. One day after setting up his experiment, it was too cloudy to proceed, so he placed his wrapped photographic plates with the uranium salt sitting on top of the plates inside a dark drawer. A few days later, he decided to develop the plates, not expecting to see anything. There were dark spots on the plates! Some form of radiation had passed through the wrappings and exposed the plates. What was the nature of these mysterious uranium rays? This intrigued Marie, and she chose this topic for her dissertation.

Her initial experiments had to be designed around the limited equipment available to her, which included the electrometer that her husband had invented. Rather quickly she found that the chemical element thorium also emitted such rays and that the intensity of the rays varied only with the quantity of thorium or uranium present. This implied that the rays originated from within the atom's interior rather than an outside source. This was her most significant scientific contribution, and it launched the field of nuclear physics. She named the emanations "radioactivity." One by one, she surveyed all the known elements as well as a variety of minerals. Pitchblende, the essential ore of uranium, was especially radioactive. After repeating some critical calculations several times over, Marie discerned that even more radioactivity emanated from the pitchblende than was possible given the small amount of uranium present in the samples. She hypothesized that another unknown and even more radioactive element must be present. She called it polonium, after her mother country, and found that it was more than 300 times more radioactive than uranium. These results were published in July 1898. Months later, it became apparent that still another stronger radioactive element was present in the pitchblende; she named it radium. This was written up and submitted to the Academy of Sciences in 1898. Radium eventually proved to be 1 million times more radioactive than polonium.

By this time, Pierre had recognized the importance of his wife's discoveries and had set aside his own work on crystals in order to assist her. In order to demonstrate the existence of a new element, a sufficient quantity had to be obtained to perform standard measurements and to determine its *atomic weight*. Using several tons of pitchblende mine waste piles obtained through the Austrian Academy of Sciences, Marie and Pierre spent four years refining a technique for isolating pure radium, 4.4 pounds (2 kg) at a time. This grueling work was physically demanding. Marie often spent entire days stirring her boiling mixture with an iron rod as tall as herself, and then it had to be distilled and electrolyzed. But neither Pierre nor Marie questioned whether their efforts were worthwhile. The principal of Pierre's school allowed the Curies to use a shed outside the school as a workplace. Though it was drafty and the roof leaked, Marie set up a pine table with her limited

**24** Science, Technology, and Society

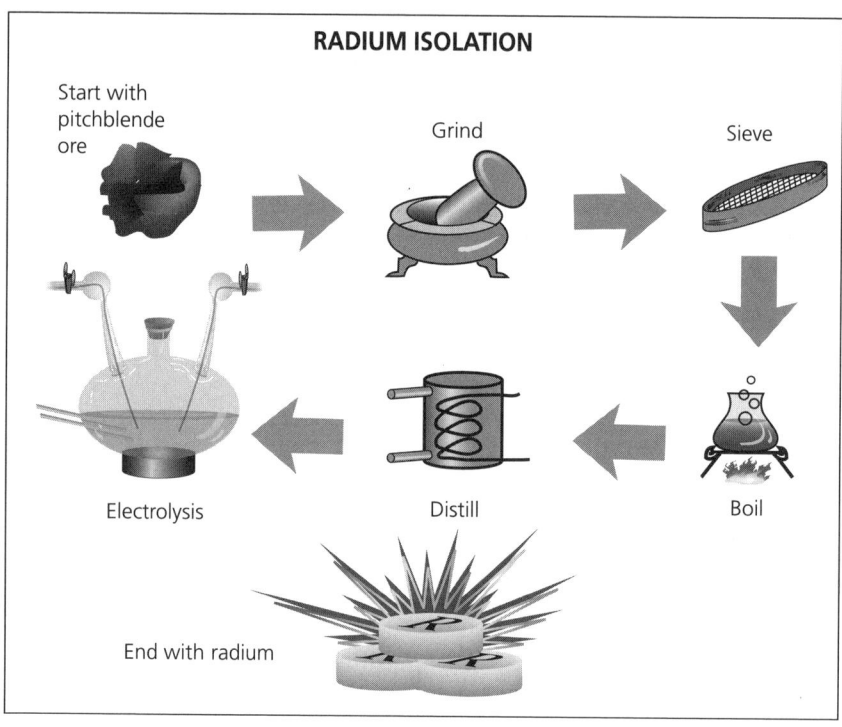

The multistep process of purifying radium was physically demanding

supply of scientific equipment and spent many years performing world-class research under these barely tolerable conditions.

As the years passed, the excitement of their discovery gave the Curies the energy necessary to continue. This took extraordinary motivation, as the work was not only physically demanding but extremely dangerous. They both began suffering from what was then an unknown danger—radiation poisoning. Their hands and fingers became burned and sore from handling the radioactivity unprotected. They were tired and dizzy. The aches in Pierre's legs were incredible, and at times he could barely stand up. But at night, after they had eaten dinner and tucked in little Irène, they went back to their primitive shed, and the little vials containing the fruits of their labor glowed a soft blue. This warm glow kept them toiling away while blinding them to the serious threat of their new precious metal.

# A Doctorate and a Nobel Prize

Finally, in March 1902, the Curies had extracted 0.0035 ounce (1 dg) of practically pure radium chloride. They determined radium to have an atomic weight of 225 (the currently accepted value is 226). The results formed her doctoral thesis, and in 1903 Marie became the first woman in Europe to receive a doctorate degree. It was a remarkable feat, yet she bettered it later that year by becoming the first woman to receive the Nobel Prize in physics, which she shared with Becquerel and her husband. In fact, there had been some disagreement on the selection committee whether a woman should be considered at all. Despite these honorable distinctions, Madame Curie remained humble. She adamantly refused to apply for a patent for the techniques used to produce radium, even though its utility in medicine was foreseen. She believed that all science and humanity should benefit from her remarkable discoveries. For her entire life, she freely shared both her knowledge and her radium.

Following the Nobel announcement, Marie and Pierre Curie's life of obscurity came to an abrupt end. The press hounded the deeply private couple, and the public curiosity caused them a great deal of stress. They were both too ill to travel to Stockholm to make the customary acceptance speech until June 1905. In 1903, Madame Curie had given birth to a stillborn baby. In 1904, she learned she was pregnant again, and recognizing her body's need to slow down, she put her research on hold until she gave birth to a healthy daughter, whom they named Eve.

Life was wonderful. Some of their financial worries had been alleviated, and public interest in their lives had settled down somewhat. They continued performing their research together, occasionally taking breaks for family trips to the country. Pierre's mother died, and his father served as caretaker for the girls so they could work without worrying whether their daughters were being provided with the best possible upbringing. Pierre was given a physics chair and promised a new laboratory at the university. He had begun examining the medicinal use of radiation in collaboration with several physicians. He found that radium killed skin cells by strapping a sample of it to his arm for a day. The result was a burn that scabbed and then scarred, suggesting that radiation could be used to destroy abnormally growing cells selectively. Within a few years the first successful cancer treatments were performed using radium generously supplied by the Curies.

## Tragedy and Scandal

Pierre never lived to see the benefits of radiation therapy, then termed *Curietherapy*. In April 1906, tragedy struck. Pierre attended a luncheon with his university colleagues and then went to visit his publisher, but no one was there. The day was rainy, and the roads were wet and muddy. He put up his umbrella and was preparing to cross the road when the rear wheel of a horse-drawn wagon struck him. He died immediately from a fractured skull. Marie was devastated by the news. She lost not only her dear husband but a devoted research partner with whom she had shared every waking moment.

Less than two weeks after his death, Marie succeeded Pierre as laboratory head and assumed his teaching duties at the Sorbonne. Once again, it was a first for a woman. That fall she started lecturing exactly where Pierre had stopped. She continued developing techniques for isolating radium. She proved to doubters that she was an extremely capable researcher and had not been riding on her husband's coattails. In 1908, she became a professor at the Sorbonne. In 1910, she published a treatise on radioactivity and because of her undisputed expertise was asked to prepare a $7 \times 10^{-5}$-ounce (2-mg) sample of radium metal to serve as an international standard. Yet when she ran for a seat in the French Academy of Sciences, she failed to receive the nomination despite her obvious merit.

By the end of 1911, a scandal broke out. There was gossip of an affair between Marie and a colleague, Paul Langevin, one of Pierre's former physics pupils. They had been close friends, and their intellectual intimacy provided a path to romance. Correspondence between the two was leaked to the press, and Langevin's wife initiated legal proceedings for custody of their four children. Though shamed and now scorned by the French public, Marie was most upset about defacing her husband's good name. Loyal friends gave her and her daughters temporary refuge until the press moved on to other matters. Interestingly, Marie and Langevin remained friends.

In the midst of her reputed scandal, Madame Curie was awarded a second Nobel Prize, this time in chemistry for her discovery of radium and polonium. While some questioned whether she deserved a second Nobel for what seemed essentially a singular achievement, chemists argued in her favor, saying that hers was the first evidence that elements transmuted. The first Nobel had been for her research on the phenomenon of radioactivity. The second was for her discovery of the chemical elements polonium and radium. This second Nobel was hers alone, and not surprisingly, she was the first person ever to receive two such awards. Madame Curie traveled to Stockholm to give her acceptance speech in December 1911.

## War Efforts

Shortly afterward, as a joint effort of the University of Paris and the Pasteur Institute, a research facility that specialized in the study of radium and its medical uses was founded in Paris. Curie served as the director for the Radium Institute. As soon as it was set up, however, World War I broke out. The French government asked Curie to hide her radium supply for fear it would get into the wrong hands and be used for destructive purposes. So the little woman lugged a 44-pound (20-kg) lead case carrying her 0.035 ounces (1 g) of radium on a train ride to Bordeaux and deposited it into a bank vault for the duration of the war.

Unable to carry out research, she did not let herself become idle. Marie became dedicated to the cause of getting radiological apparatuses onto the battlefields to expedite surgeries for removing bullets and shrapnel from wounded soldiers. She toured to collect finances and vehicles and by the end of the war had assembled 20 mobile X-ray units. With her 18-year-old daughter Irène's assistance, she trained hundreds of doctors and orderlies in the operation of the units and set up more than 200 X-ray clinics. More than 1 million soldiers benefited from her efforts.

After the war, the Radium Institute opened, and under Madame Curie's direction it became a premier research institution, though its facilities were modest by American standards. She served as its director until her death. Due to the increased usage of radium in cancer treatments, which was amazingly successful, she received numerous requests for samples of the radium that she worked so hard to collect. She could not refuse anyone. After a while her radium supply was diminished, and she did not have enough money to buy more, at a cost of approximately $100,000 per 0.035 ounce (1 g). An American journalist, Marie (Missy) Maloney, heard of Curie's plight and was shocked to learn that the discoverer of radium had none for herself, while labs across America were well-stocked with more than 1.8 ounces (50 g). Maloney vowed to campaign to supply her with 0.035 ounce (1 g) of radium. In 1921, Curie traveled to the United States to receive the gift in person from President Warren Harding. The donation followed weeks of receptions and celebrations in her honor. She received honorary doctorate degrees from Yale and Columbia. Unfortunately, Curie's visit was abbreviated because her health was deteriorating.

### The Nobel Prize in Chemistry 1935

In 1935, Irène Joliot-Curie and Frédéric Joliot-Curie shared the Nobel Prize in chemistry for their synthesis of new radioactive elements. At the time, Nobel Prizes for research on radioactivity already had been presented to Henri Becquerel, Marie Curie, and Pierre Curie jointly (1903), Ernest Rutherford (1908), Marie Curie (1911), and Frederick Soddy (1922). Research on this phenomenon had led to a new method for treating cancer, determination of the minimum age of the Earth, and insight into the structure and internal energy of the atom. Three spontaneous radioactive decay series were known, two from radium and one from thorium, and more than 40 natural radioactive elements had been identified from these series. Radioactivity was indeed a popular topic.

The Joliot-Curie research team successfully transformed one element into another by external interference, in contrast with radioactive elements that formed by spontaneous decay. Transformation can occur by

After recovering enough strength to return to work, she continued giving lectures, raising money and recruiting scientists for the Radium Institute of Paris. In 1929, she traveled to the United States once more to receive an additional 0.035 ounce (1 g) of radium for the Radium Institute that had opened in Warsaw. By this time, the dangers of radiation exposure were apparent. X-ray technicians and scientists who worked with radium were suffering, as were women who worked painting watch dials with radium to make them glow.

## Death from Cancer

Curie's own health worsened. She was practically blind despite several operations for cataracts. She heard constant humming in her ears and suffered unexplained fevers. She was weak and frail. With

the collision of subatomic particles called alpha particles, which consist of helium atoms with positive electrical charges, with the nucleus of other atoms. The nucleus is so tiny, however, that the chance of collision without assistance is infinitesimal. The Joliot-Curies bombarded aluminum with alpha particles from polonium, which Marie Curie had discovered. Polonium was a good choice for this task, since it is very unstable and therefore emits a plentitude of alpha particles at high speeds, increasing the chances of successful collisions. Following bombardment, the aluminum itself began emitting rays, proving it had become radioactive. Analysis showed it had been transformed into a radioactive isotope of phosphorus. They also successfully transformed boron into radioactive nitrogen and magnesium into radioactive silicon and radioactive aluminum. The radioactive elements that they created subsequently decomposed spontaneously.

Practical uses of artificial radioactivity include new sources of gamma radiation, the use of radioactive isotopes for tracing the movement of atoms through biochemical pathways, and the treatment of cancer. Their discovery made possible the artificial transformation of one element into another, for the benefit of pure science, physicians, and the rest of humanity.

her daughter Eve at her bedside, on July 4, 1934, she passed away from leukemia, brought on by years of exposure to radioactivity. She was 66 years old. After her coffin was placed on top of her husband's in a cemetery in Sceaux, her sister Bronia and her brother Josef dropped handfuls of dirt from her beloved Poland into her grave. Even after her death, Madame Curie had another first. In 1995, President François Mitterrand of France oversaw the reburial of her remains at the Panthéon in Paris. She was the first woman to be honored this way on her own merit.

Sadly, she did not live to see her daughter, Irène Joliot-Curie, and her son-in-law, Frédéric Joliot-Curie, receive the Nobel Prize in chemistry for their discovery of *artificial radiation*. Whereas Madame Curie studied elements that were naturally radioactive, the Joliot-Curie research team discovered a method to create radioactive isotopes of elements. The news of the award was announced just months after Curie's death. Today artificial radiation is of immeasurable value to all sorts of scientists, from biochemists to mineralogists.

From Marya Skłodowska, a tiny, shy, Polish immigrant girl, to the brilliant, proud, stubborn, dedicated, pioneering researcher Madame Doctor Marie Curie, her legacy persists today. Every person who has had a loved one successfully treated with radiation therapy owes gratitude to Marie Curie. X-rays performed to diagnose a broken bone or locate a cavity are possible because of her discoveries. Nuclear power plants that produce energy are the descendants of her researches, as are nuclear weapons. (Interestingly, in the delayed acceptance speech for the shared Nobel Prize in physics, Pierre warned about the possible dangerous uses of radiation and nuclear power.) Marie Curie lived to advance science for the sake of knowledge itself. She believed the benefits outweighed the possible dangers, though she gave her life in the efforts to prove so. One hundred years later, society benefits because of her hard work.

## CHRONOLOGY

| | |
|---|---|
| 1867 | Marya Skłodowska is born on November 7 in Warsaw, Poland |
| 1886 | Starts work as a governess |

| | |
|---|---|
| 1891 | Moves to Paris to study at the Sorbonne |
| 1893 | Obtains a physics degree; is first in her class |
| 1894 | Obtains a mathematics degree; is second in her class |
| 1895 | Becomes lab assistant to Pierre Curie |
| 1896 | Begins work on radioactivity |
| 1898 | Presents first paper to *Academie des Sciences,* discovers polonium, and announces discovery of radium |
| 1902 | Distills pure radium and determines its atomic weight |
| 1903 | Earns a doctorate degree in physics. Pierre and Marie Curie each share one-fourth of the Nobel Prize in physics in recognition of their extraordinary research on the radiation phenomena discovered by Henri Becquerel, who received the other half of the Nobel that year |
| 1904 | Publishes *Researches on Radioactive Substances* |
| 1906 | Pierre dies, and Marie becomes the first woman to lecture at the Sorbonne |
| 1908 | Becomes the first female professor at the Sorbonne |
| 1910 | Isolates metallic radium |
| 1911 | Provides radium sample for international standard and receives the Nobel Prize in chemistry in recognition of her discovery of the elements radium and polonium and the isolation and study of the nature and compounds of radium |
| 1912 | Becomes director of the Radium Institute in Paris |
| 1914–18 | Organizes mobile X-ray units and trains operators for the French army |
| 1934 | Her daughter Irène and her son-in-law, Frédéric, discover artificial radioactivity |
| 1934 | Dies of leukemia on July 4 |

## FURTHER READING

Giroud, Françoise. *Marie Curie: A Life.* Translated by Lydia Davis. New York: Holmes and Meier, 1986. Standard biography that attempts to portray the complex personality of Curie.

Meadows, Jack. *The Great Scientists: The Story of Science Told Through the Lives of Twelve Landmark Figures.* New York: Oxford University Press, 1987. Brief biographies of 12 high-profile scientists and the development of science as influenced by social forces. Colorful illustrations.

Nobleprize.org. "The Nobel Prize in Physics 1903." Available online. URL: http://www.nobelprize.org/physics/laureates/1903. Last modified on June 16, 2000. Includes biography, article, and other references, including links to the Web site for her Nobel Prize in chemistry in 1911.

Pflaum, Rosalynd. *Marie Curie and Her Daughter Irène.* Minneapolis, Minn.: Lerner Publications, 1993. Presents the life stories of Marie Curie, discoverer of radium and polonium, and her daughter, Irène Joliot-Curie, discoverer of artificial radiation. Appropriate for middle and high school students.

Saari, Peggy, and Stephen Allison, eds. *The Lives and Works of 150 Scientists.* Vol. 1. Detroit: U*X*L, 1996. Alphabetically arranged introductions to the contributions of scientists from a variety of fields. Intended for middle school students.

# Guglielmo Marconi

## (1874–1937)

Guglielmo Marconi invented the first practical system of wireless telegraphy. *(Library of Congress, Prints and Photographs Division [LC-USZ62-77563])*

## The First Transatlantic Radio Transmission

In today's world, people can communicate long distances instantaneously. One can call from and to almost anywhere on the Earth through the use of cell phones. Satellites transmit real-time coverage of the war in the Middle East to televisions in the United States. Instant messaging friends is possible through the Internet. Before the 19th century, the only means of communicating over distances farther than the eye could see involved human travel. In 1837, American Samuel Morse invented a telegraph machine that used an electromagnet to click out short or long sounds representing letters and numbers. Later he adapted it to print out dots and dashes onto paper. Messages in Morse code could be sent through electrical wires, even underwater across the Atlantic after 1858. The first telephone system that allowed speech to be transmitted electrically was created in 1877, and in 1883 telephones connected cities, but this required wires to connect the phones directly. Cellular phones did not become available until the early 1980s.

Almost a century beforehand, one man dreamed of being able to link the entire world without the use of connecting wires. Though the principles he used and applied were widely researched among the scientists of that time, no one had integrated the knowledge into society before the young Italian physicist Guglielmo Marconi. Marconi's work led to today's world of wireless communications, which link ships and planes to shore and send television and *radio* signals into outer space and back. Invisible waves surround the Earth.

## An Early Interest in Physics

Guglielmo Marconi was born on April 25, 1874, to Giuseppe Marconi and his Irish wife, Annie Jameson. She was his second wife, and they already had one nine-year-old son, named Alfonso, as well as Giuseppe's first son, Luigi, from his former wife, who had died during childbirth. The Marconis owned a house in the city of Bologna, Italy, as well as a country summer home, Villa Griffone, 10.6 miles (17 km) away in Pontecchio. Giuseppe was a shrewd businessman and landowner who farmed his lands on a sharecropping system and preferred to stay near his fields by the villa. He had a decent library, where young Guglielmo independently explored Greek mythology and the sciences. Annie and the boys traveled seasonally because Annie's delicate health could not tolerate the cold of Bologna during the winter months. They often spent winters at Leghorn, Italy, on the western edge of Tuscany, where Annie's sister and her family lived. Guglielmo attended private schools and had private tutors, but he was not a very diligent student nor was he very popular. In 1887, he entered the Leghorn Technical Institute, where he was exposed to more scientific disciplines. There he fell in love with physics.

The young man's mother was very encouraging and supported his hobby by hiring a private physics teacher for her son. Guglielmo began experimenting at home and eventually set up his own laboratory in the attic of Villa Griffone using makeshift equipment and old tools from his grandfather's silkworm business. He reportedly converted his young cousin's sewing machine into a meat roaster turnspit. Supposedly this made her cry, so Guglielmo converted it back again. Unfortunately, his enthusiasm for physics caused his performance in his other school subjects to suffer, and he never received his diploma. His father was not pleased, but Annie managed to keep Giuseppe calm enough to allow Guglielmo the freedom to continue his explorations. She also arranged his introduction to Augusto Righi, a physics professor at the University of Bologna, where Guglielmo could never be admitted due to his poor academic record. Righi was impressed with the budding scientist and permitted him access to his own laboratory and the university's library. From time to time, Guglielmo would seek the professor's assistance in understanding a theory or explanation of a particular experiment's results.

Guglielmo was particularly interested in electricity. He was fascinated by Benjamin Franklin's *Experiments and Observations on Electricity*, which was published in 1751, and by Michael Faraday's lectures on electricity at the Royal Institution of London. He searched the library to learn even more. He attempted to replicate many of the experiments he read about and soon began executing original experiments. He became so absorbed in his researches that he would skip meals if not for his mother, who brought him trays up to the attic. His disapproving father viewed this as mindless fiddling and failed to see the productivity in his son's work. By now Guglielmo was 19 years old, and Giuseppe thought he should be making plans for a career and his future. So when Guglielmo started requesting money to buy supplies and equipment for his researches, his stern father was not especially pleased, but under Annie's persuasion he submitted.

# Invention of the Wireless Telegraph

In 1894, Guglielmo began experimenting with wireless telegraphy. He had read an article written by Righi that summarized the research of the German physicist Heinrich Hertz (1857–94), who had died earlier that year. Hertz had developed equipment that produced an oscillating electrical circuit. The circuit jumped from one metal knob to another close by, then rapidly (thousands of times per second) changed direction and jumped back and forth continuously, in the process producing a spark between the two knobs. Decades before, Scottish physicist James Clerk Maxwell had mathematically proposed that such an oscillating current would generate very long *electromagnetic waves* as a result of the electrical discharge. Hertz devised

### Electromagnetic Waves

Marconi's invention relied on electromagnetic waves to transmit signals across distances without the use of wires. What is the nature of electromagnetic waves? Positively charged protons attract negatively charged electrons. A force field exists in the area surrounding a proton, and if an electron lands anywhere in this force field, it will be pulled toward the proton. If another proton were placed in the field, it would be repelled. Lines of force can be imagined by picturing the direction that the attractive force would extend toward electrons placed anywhere in the force field. If an electron were moved up or down within the force field, the invisible line of force extending between the two particles would wiggle like the waves that are created by wiggling a rope held stretched out between two people. These vibrations through space are called electromagnetic waves.

Electromagnetic waves are a form of energy that can travel through water, air, or even a vacuum. They are measured in wavelength, which

a contraption to detect the presence of electromagnetic waves. The detection device was simply a single wire loop that contained a tiny gap. The radiation produced by the oscillating spark in the *transmitter* induced a spark in the gap of the wire loop from a distance of several yards. Hertz proved the waves had *wavelengths* of slightly greater than two feet (61 cm) and had both electric and magnetic fields. Though Righi advised Marconi not to get overly excited about these Hertzian waves, Marconi could not help but be amazed. He believed that such waves could be used to communicate without the use of connecting wires as were used for telegraph and telephone signals. In fact, he could not believe it had not already been done.

In his attic lab, Marconi gathered metal bits, sheets of copper, and wires and tried to replicate Hertz's experiments. He built an

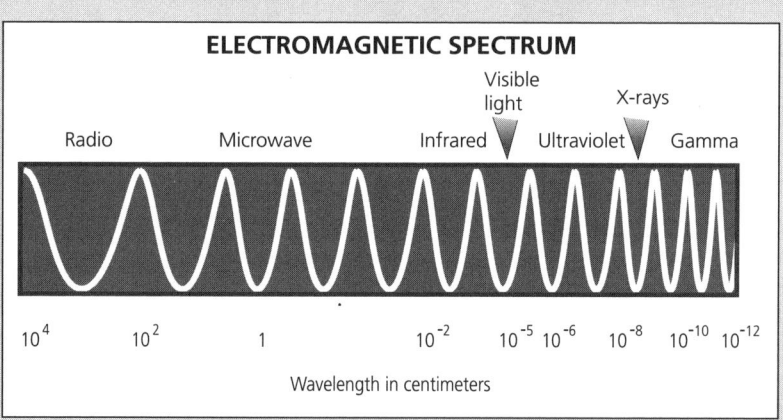

The electromagnetic spectrum ranges in wavelength from less than one nanometer to more than one kilometer.

describes the distance between the peaks of two individual waves and is indicative of the amount of energy present in the waves. The faster the charge vibrates, the shorter the wavelength, and the higher energy the wave has. As *frequency* (the number of complete waves that pass through a point in a given time period) increases, the wavelength decreases, and vice versa. All electromagnetic waves travel at the speed of light (about 186,000 miles or 300,000 km per second).

induction coil to make high-voltage sparks. He made a few alterations, including putting a piece of curved metal behind the transmitter. He also substituted a *coherer*, which consisted of two electrodes separated by a glass tube filled with metal filings in place of the copper wire loop, as a *receiver*. In the presence of electromagnetic radiation produced by the sparks in the transmitter, the pieces of metal in the glass tube would all stick together, or cohere, allowing the current to pass through. Marconi connected this coherer to an electric bell that would ding when the current was allowed to pass. Next he connected a telegraph key to the transmitter. When the key was pressed, it sent a current of electricity that passed through wires of an induction coil to *amplify* the current, then to the metal balls, which emitted an oscillatory spark across the gap. The spark caused electromagnetic vibrations to travel through the air in all directions, and the ones that reached the coherer rang the bell. It worked! Marconi was thrilled. He made modifications such as using larger antennas and adding metal plates to the balls to increase the signal strength until he was able to transmit the signals nine yards (8.2 m) across the length of his attic laboratory, then woke his mother up in the middle of one night in 1895 to demonstrate his triumph. While Annie might not have recognized the significance of his discovery, she did recognize her son's wild enthusiasm and excitement. But Giuseppe was not as easily impressed. He still worried that his son spent too much time in seclusion.

Marconi adapted the coherer to make what he named a decoherer. The coherer required resetting by manually tapping on the glass tube after each signal was received to unstick the metal filings. Marconi improved this device by including a tiny electromagnet-operated hammer that gently struck the side of the tube after the circuit passed through. This meant he did not need to keep running to the other side of the room and could send several signals without pause. He also experimented with the metal powder mixture within the tube. He found that a combination of 95 percent nickel and 5 percent silver worked optimally.

Additional improvements allowed Marconi to move his receiver outside the house. The bell still rang. Marconi had been using four metal balls, but now replaced two of them with sheet iron, adding

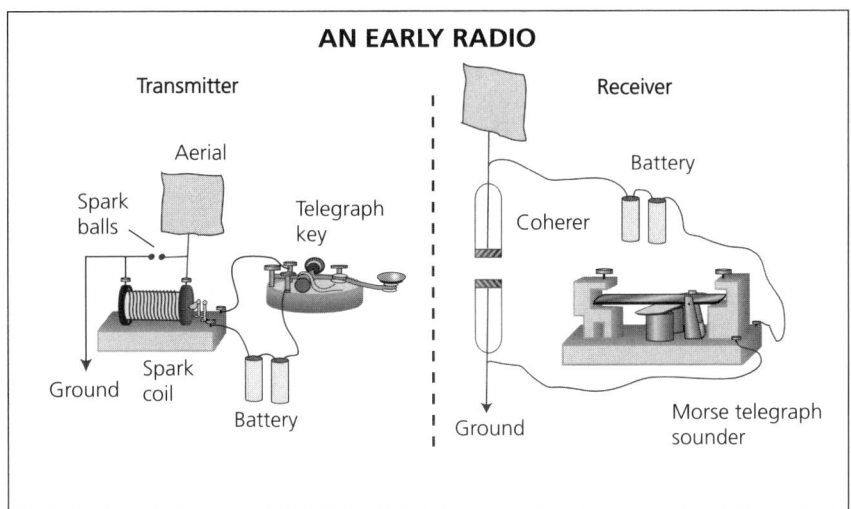

Diagram of an early radio transmitter and receiver

iron sheets to the receiver as well, and lifted one of the metal sheets high above the ground. He tested different combinations of tube shapes and positions of the coherer and tried different positions for the antennas. By September 1895, he could transmit intelligible signals up to one-half mile (805 m). He linked aerial copper wires to his transmitter and put copper wires in the ground. Then he added aerial and ground wires to his receiver, increasing his signals to more than one mile (1.6 km). At one point he noticed that the signals seemed to travel through hills. To test this he sent his rifle-toting brother Alfonso to observe a receiver over a hill one and one-half miles (2.4 km) away. If Alfonso heard the bell ring, he was to shoot. When Marconi tapped the Morse key, his brother responded with a gunshot!

Now his father took notice, but greater funding than Giuseppe could provide was necessary to build a larger transmitter. They wrote the Italian post office, describing Marconi's success with the wireless telegraph, but the government either did not recognize the implications or perhaps had no faith in this barely educated 21-year-old amateur. So in early 1896, Guglielmo and Annie Marconi traveled to England, where Annie had relatives, in hopes of obtaining financial assistance. One of Annie's nephews was an engineer, and with his assistance Marconi registered his first patent for a wireless telegraph. Marconi was also put into contact with the engineer in chief of the British Post Office, William Preece. Preece was one of the first telegraph engineers and was very anxious to speak with Marconi concerning his claims of being able to transmit wireless radio signals across distances of more than one mile (1.6 km).

Marconi's demonstration to Preece was impressive. It was followed by a series of public demonstrations to larger audiences. By now Marconi had replaced his bell with a Morse printing machine. Preece had also given Marconi an assistant, George Stevens Kemp, who would remain his assistant and friend until his death. Meanwhile, Marconi continued making improvements by experimenting with the heights and angles of the aerials. In March 1897, he sent a signal four miles (6.4 km). In May 1897, he sent a signal about 10 miles (16 km) from the British mainland to an island in the British Channel.

About this time, Italy realized its mistake in ignoring Marconi's earlier plea for assistance. The Italian government invited Marconi for a demonstration, and in July 1897 the first ship-to-shore signal was sent from an Italian navy ship. This was amazing, because people assumed that the curvature of the Earth would prevent signals from being received from a ship below the optical horizon. They assumed the electromagnetic waves would either travel up into space or be absorbed into the Earth. Marconi was of the age where all Italian men were required to serve in the military for three years. The Italian king waived Marconi's liability for military service by arranging a position at the Italian embassy in London for Marconi so he would not have to interrupt his exciting research. Marconi anonymously sent his military paychecks to an Italian hospital in London.

# Demonstration of the Utility of Wireless Telegraphy

In 1897, Marconi turned his scientific success into commercial success by founding a communications company, the Wireless Telegraph and Signal Company, Ltd. (later to be renamed Marconi's Wireless Telegraph Company, Ltd.), whose goal was to set up permanent wireless stations around Britain. The following year, Marconi reported updates on the Kingstown Regatta yacht races from a tugboat following the yachts to the shore where the local newspaper received and reported them. Britain's Queen Victoria was in Dublin and very anxious to hear the results. This reporting piqued the interest of the general public in radio technology. In 1898, the Prince of Wales (the future King Edward VII) had injured his knee and was staying on board the Royal Yacht. Marconi was asked to install equipment that would permit communications between the Royal yacht and Osborne House, where Queen Victoria was staying. Over a 16-day period, the prince and his mother sent more than 150 messages to each other without any problems. In March 1899, the first international wireless signals were sent 32 miles (51.5 km) across the English Channel, from Dover, England, to Wimereux, France, and later that year Marconi reported on the America's Cup yacht race. The public already considered Marconi a magician, but he became a hero when a worker fell overboard a battleship and wireless telegraphy communicated the emergency to a rescue boat.

Though he was able to send signals consistently more than 60 miles (97 km) now, Marconi was troubled by the problem of interference. In order for wireless telegraphy to take off commercially, he had to be able to limit the range of frequencies sent and received by specific stations. Without being able to do this, receiving a comprehensible radiotelegraph would be as difficult as trying to watch one television show among hundreds of television shows viewed simultaneously on a single channel. His determination led him eventually to develop a mechanism for selective tuning to different frequencies. His next immediate goal was to transmit a wireless signal across the ocean.

## Successful Transatlantic Transmission

His team fashioned a transmitting station 100 times more powerful than any previously built, on the cliffs of the coast at Poldhu, in Cornwall, England. They set up a receiving antenna across the

Atlantic Ocean, 1,800 miles (2,900 km) away in Cape Cod, Massachusetts. At such a distance the hump between the two stations caused by the Earth's natural curvature was more than 50 miles (80 km) high, and most scientists did not believe that wireless signals would be able to overcome this obstacle. New specially designed equipment was built, including aerials almost 40 feet (12 m) high, but in September 1901 strong winds destroyed the set-ups in Poldhu. They were replaced with a simpler design. Then in November, the antenna towers in Cape Cod were blown over during a storm. Frustration grew, but Marconi remained calm. To maintain secrecy, he moved his receiving equipment to Newfoundland off the east coast of Canada. By that December they were prepared for the first trials. Despite weather interference and losing at least one kite and one balloon to sea, Marconi prevailed. With the kite-mounted antenna lifted 400 feet (122 m), a few weak but unmistakable signals of three dots representing the Morse letter *S* were received across the 2,100-mile (3,380-km) distance! Marconi had successfully transmitted and received the first wireless transatlantic communication, his most famous accomplishment. Marconi knew sturdy, permanent aerial antennas were needed. Unfortunately, the local telegraph company in Newfoundland was jealous and feared losing cabled business to the new wireless systems. They threatened to sue Marconi for infringing on their rights to all telegraphy in the area. So Marconi moved out.

Another station was set up at Glace Bay, Cape Breton Island, Nova Scotia. During all the back and forth travels between Great Britain and Nova Scotia making plans and gathering equipment and personnel, Marconi collected invaluable data. He found that signals were clearer at night. At the time the reason was not understood but was later found to be due to the *ionosphere*. In December 1902, lucid signals were received from Poldhu at Glace Bay, proving that the Earth's curvature was not an obstacle for radio waves. Scientists later determined that a region of the Earth's upper atmosphere called the ionosphere helps keep signals on track despite the Earth's curvature. The ionosphere is a layer of gas particles charged by the Sun's radiation. It reflects or bounces any wave signals that reach it back to the Earth. Signals traveling across the Atlantic bounce back and forth between the Earth and the ionosphere many times before they lose power. During daylight the density of the ionized layer is altered and not as suitable for reflection as during nighttime. This explains the increased reception distance at nighttime.

Marconi continued experimenting to improve his equipment in order to receive consistently clear signals. In 1902, he replaced the coherer with a device he invented called a magnetic detector. One of his engineers invented a multiple tuner device that facilitated tuning to specific wavelengths. In 1905, Marconi started using a horizontal directional aerial that greatly enhanced reception.

Meanwhile, personally, Marconi was considered quite a ladies' man. He did settle down in 1905, when he married Beatrice O'Brien, with whom he had one son and two daughters. However, they divorced in 1924, and he later became estranged from his former wife and children.

In recognition of the advancements made in wireless telegraphy, Marconi was awarded the Nobel Prize in physics in 1909, an honor he shared with the German physicist Karl Ferdinand Braun. Though some questioned why Marconi had to share the prize, the two men became friends.

During the next few decades Marconi led his company in making continual gradual improvements in the technology used to send wireless signals. The masses not only continued to be amazed but also began to depend on his wireless systems. He proved his systems were practical and reliable and gained much public support for radio technology. In 1904, the first ship-to-shore communication system was established with the Cunard steamship line. In 1909, a cruise liner crossing the Atlantic crashed into another ship and suffered severe damage. However, the wireless operator turned on the emergency batteries and sent a wireless signal to shore for help. Wireless signals guided the way to the downed liner, and 1,700 lives were saved. On April 15, 1912, the *Titanic* crashed into an iceberg despite wireless warnings of ice in the area, and 1,500 travelers died due to a deficient number of lifeboats. Wireless calls for help were sent out, but the wireless operator on the nearest ship, which could have saved more than the 700 lucky survivors, was temporarily off duty. Other ships were receiving other messages at the time, which prevented the SOS from coming through. A ship farther away did respond, but it was too late for the victims.

After this tragic incident, radio equipment was installed on most ships, and the stations were continually manned.

The same year as the sinking of the *Titanic*, Marconi himself suffered personal tragedy when he injured his right eye in a car accident. He lost his sight in that eye and later in life wore a glass eye.

Wireless antennas in Maryland during the 1920s *(Courtesy of the family of Thomas D. Whitely)*

During World War I (1914–18), Marconi served as a technical consultant for the Italian military. In 1916, while in the hospital with a sore throat, he began to experiment with the use of shortwaves (having wavelengths of approximately 10 feet or 3 m) to transmit electrical signals. Shorter electromagnetic waves did not require such large aerials and were easier to direct. In 1920, Marconi bought a ship he christened the *Elettra* that he transformed into a floating 200-foot (61-m) laboratory as well as temporary home. Around 1922 his company started a new Imperial Wireless System, and by 1927 the Earth was completely encircled with shortwave wireless communication systems. Marconi was still only 52 years old.

After having his first marriage annulled, Marconi married his second wife, Countess Maria Christina Bezzi-Scali, in 1927. They had one daughter named Elettra, after his yacht, in 1930. He returned to Italy and suffered several heart attacks over the next decade. Nevertheless, he broke new ground in the 1930s by researching microwaves, which are less than 0.39 inch (1 cm) long. Microwaves require less power to send great distances because the ionosphere reflects them very efficiently. Marconi showed that these waves could be easily directed by using an antenna shaped like a dish. He also demonstrated that they were useful for navigating ships through fog. Later, microwaves became the foundation for research in developing Radar (radio detecting and ranging), which can detect positions of distant objects and phenomena. Today radar is used for a variety of applications, such as safely navigating airplanes and ships, as well as in weather forecasting.

## The Father of Radio

The father of radio died of a heart attack at age 63, in Rome, on July 20, 1937. He was given a state funeral by the Italian government and was buried in Bologna. The news of his death was spread around the world by wireless and two minutes of radio silence were observed in his honor. This was a fitting tribute to the man who united the world by wireless communication.

During his lifetime Marconi received numerous medals and honors in addition to his Nobel Prize in physics. In 1929, he was made a nobleman by the Italian government and given the title of marchese. He was given several other titles and appointments by other countries as well, including England and Russia. He was awarded honorary doctorate degrees and numerous medals. Yet despite all the recognition for his ingenuity and the utility of his inventions, Marconi would no doubt be amazed at the modern applications of his technological advances. Perhaps he would even be tickled that people use microwaves to heat up frozen pizza and cell phones so they may call home to ask for a ride after soccer practice.

Marconi was not formally trained in science. He was largely self-educated and performed all his early work in an attic room that his grandfather had used for breeding silkworms. He worked through many failures and disappointments to reach his ultimate success. He once told his daughter, "Genius, if you like to call it that, is the gift of work continuously applied," words he lived by (Gunston 84). While he did not discover electromagnetic radiation, he was the first to dedicate himself to using electromagnetic waves to transmit intelligible electrical signals without the use of directly connecting wires. Sometimes the most profound scientific discoveries are not made in theory or basic research but in discovering how to apply natural phenomena to improve the lives of mankind. Because of Marconi's determination to turn his vision into tangible reality, we live in a safer, more productive, exciting, and entertaining world.

## CHRONOLOGY

| | |
|---|---|
| 1874 | Guglielmo Marconi is born on April 25 in Bologna, Italy |
| 1887 | Enters the Leghorn Technical Institute |
| 1894 | Begins experimenting with electromagnetic waves |
| 1895 | Invents the decoherer and sends the first signal 1.5 miles (2.4 km) at Villa Griffone |
| 1896 | Marconi and his mother travel to England, where he applies for his first patent for radiotelegraphy. He performs the first public trial of wireless telegraphy in London and sends a signal over two miles (3.2 km) in Salisbury Plain, England |

| | |
|---|---|
| 1897 | Sends the first ship-to-shore wireless signal over a distance of 12 miles (19.3) and founds the Wireless Telegraph and Signal Company, Ltd. |
| 1899 | Sends a wireless signal across the English Channel |
| 1900–12 | Patents several new improvements to wireless |
| 1901 | Sends the first transatlantic wireless signal from Britain to Canada |
| 1909 | Wireless telegraphy saves 1,700 people from a shipwreck. Marconi is awarded the Nobel Prize in physics with Karl Ferdinand Braun |
| 1912 | Wireless communication saves the *Titanic* survivors |
| 1913–18 | Undertakes diplomatic missions for Italy during and after World War I |
| 1916 | Begins experimenting with short radio waves |
| 1927 | Shortwave beam stations circle the globe |
| 1929 | Receives the title marchese by the Italian government |
| 1932 | Directs microwaves with a dish antenna and discovers that microwaves can be received far below the horizon |
| 1934 | Demonstrates the use of microwaves for navigation through fog |
| 1935 | Demonstrates the principles of radar |
| 1937 | Dies in Rome on July 20 at age 63 |

## FURTHER READING

Birch, Beverley. *Guglielmo Marconi: Radio Pioneer.* Woodbridge, Conn.: Blackbirch Press, 2001. The life and work of the Italian inventor written for juvenile readers.

Gillispie, Charles C., ed. *Dictionary of Scientific Biography.* Vol. 9. New York: Scribner, 1970–76. Good source for facts concerning personal background and scientific accomplishments but assumes reader has basic knowledge of science.

Gunston, David. *Marconi: Father of Radio.* New York: Crowell-Collier Press, 1967. Standard biography written for young adults.

Masini, Giancarlo. *Marconi.* New York: Marsilio Publishers, 1976. Describes life, experiments, and achievements of Marconi.

Nobelprize.org. "The Nobel Prize in Physics 1909." Available online. URL: http://www.nobelprize.org/physics/laureates/1909. Last modified on June 16, 2000. Includes biography, lecture, banquet speech, and links to other references.

Olson, Richard, ed. *Biographical Encyclopedia of Scientists.* Vol. 4. New York: Marshall Cavendish, 1998. Contains brief biographies, including time lines of significant events.

# Sir Frederick G. Banting

(1891–1941)

Sir Frederick G. Banting discovered insulin in a hot, cramped, borrowed lab space in the early 1920s.
(© *The Nobel Foundation*)

## Discoverer of Insulin

The International Diabetes Federation estimates that almost 200 million people in the world have *diabetes*, a disease in which the body does not efficiently utilize sugar due to an inability to produce or utilize *insulin*. Without insulin, an excess of glucose collects in the bloodstream and is excreted in the urine, and the body does not obtain the energy it needs, leading to a cruel death by slow starvation. For the victims of diabetes whose bodies cannot make insulin, injections of the hormone help regulate the levels of sugar in the blood, and the afflicted can live a practically normal life. Canadian physician Sir Frederick Banting is venerated for his discovery of insulin and its utility as a treatment for diabetes. Today, millions of diabetics can expect to live normal, useful lives due to his determination in finding a treatment for a disease that had been labeled as hopeless.

## Farm Boy Becomes Military Surgeon

Frederick Grant Banting was born to William and Margaret Banting on November 14, 1891, in Alliston, Ontario. He was the youngest of five children and grew up in a deeply religious household on a farm. An average student and a decent athlete, he spent his childhood exploring around the farm and its riverbank with his cousin and their tomboy friend Jane. At age 14, his playmate Jane suddenly became gravely ill; she became as thin as a paper doll, lost all her energy, and died of a mysterious illness called diabetes. Unknown at the time, this memorable event would have a tremendous impact on the course Fred would pursue in his future.

After graduating from the local public school in 1910, he enrolled at Victoria College, a liberal arts institution in Toronto. Fred's father dreamed of his youngest son becoming a minister. Not wanting to disappoint his parents, Fred planned on majoring in theology, but once he arrived at school, he felt guilty knowing he was wasting time studying for something in which he was not truly interested. While visiting home during the spring of 1912, he admitted to his parents that he was most fascinated with medicine. The following autumn, he registered as a medical student at the University of Toronto. Banting was much happier as a medical student, and he scrimped and saved to purchase his own microscope, which cost $57.50, a fortune in those days. He spent his free time studying his own blood under the microscope, perfecting his tissue preparation techniques, and even conducting his own experiments in the laboratory.

Under the tutelage of the surgeon-in-chief for the nearby Hospital for Sick Children, Dr. Clarence L. Starr, Banting decided to specialize in orthopedic surgery, the surgical correction of skeletal deformities. After World War I broke out in 1914, licensed doctors were scarce in the city, and once, when none were available, Banting was granted special permission to perform a tonsillectomy. The medical students' courses were accelerated, and many were anxious to show their patriotism by joining the military. They graduated six months early, in December 1916, and Banting immediately entered the Canadian Army Medical Corps as a lieutenant.

Banting first went to England but was anxious to be closer to the fighting. He soon received his wish and was sent to France, where he witnessed the suffering of many wounded soldiers and obtained lots of surgical experience. In 1918, Banting was injured by a piece of shrapnel that severed an artery and almost split his right forearm in two. With a tourniquet on his arm, he disobeyed orders from his major and continued dressing the wounds of other soldiers for 17 hours. The doctors wanted to amputate, but he refused to let them. He determinedly strove to rehabilitate his arm, a slow and painful process, and received the Military Cross for his brave conduct during action.

## Repairing Childhood Deformities

In 1919, Banting returned to Toronto, where he accepted an orthopedic surgery position under his mentor, Starr, at the Hospital for Sick Children. He specialized in the mechanical correction of childhood deformities such as clubfeet and twisted limbs. Though awkward and shy with his peers, he felt at ease with the children he treated. After one year, he attempted to start his own surgical practice in London, Ontario.

Banting was unable to attract patients, so to earn money, he accepted a part-time instructorship in anatomy, physiology, and clinical surgery for the medical school at Western University (now the University of Western Ontario). Banting was popular with students and prepared his lectures with care, always taking time to ensure he included the latest reports and discoveries. He missed performing medical research and often joined the chief of physiology, Dr. Frederick R. Miller, in his neurophysiologic investigations. Together the physicians showed that the cortex of the brain was sensitive to outside stimulation. These studies rekindled Banting's interest in experimentation.

## Hormone X

Banting spent a lot of time in the library reading medical journals and preparing his lectures. In the autumn of 1920, he began preparing for an upcoming lecture on the *pancreas*, a large abdominal gland that produces digestive juices. The juices contain enzymes that travel through a *duct* to the small intestine, where they chemically break down proteins, lipids, and carbohydrates into simpler molecules that the body can readily absorb. Removal of the pancreas led to increased levels of sugar in the blood and urine, and death resulted. Banting searched the medical literature to learn more about this gland.

Banting found descriptions of diabetes symptoms dating 4,000 years ago. The disease is characterized by unquenchable thirst and hunger, high sugar levels in the blood and urine, an acetone-like odor on the breath, tiredness and depression, extreme weight loss, and, eventually, a coma leading to death. Though the disease had been recognized since ancient times, no treatment or cure had been discovered. Banting wondered why so little was known about treating diabetes.

In 1869, a medical student named Paul Langerhans noticed clumps of dark spots in pancreatic tissue. These groups of cells, later named *islets of Langerhans*, looked different than the regular pancreatic cells that secreted digestive enzymes, and they did not lead to the small intestine via a duct. In 1889, the German researchers Josef von Mehring and Oskar Minkowksi removed the pancreas of a dog, which subsequently developed acute diabetes mellitus and died within two weeks. The islets of Langerhans in the pancreatic tissue from deceased diabetics appeared atrophied. Some scientists thought an unknown hormone that was absorbed by the body in mysterious ways was produced by these cells and that it helped the body burn sugar for energy. Several physicians, including Dr. John James Richard Macleod (1876–1935), the head of physiology at the University of Toronto, claimed that there was no proof of the existence of this unknown "hormone X."

On the evening of October 30, 1920, the day before Banting's lecture on the pancreas, he visited the library one last time to search for additional material to include in his lecture. That morning, a new issue of the journal *Surgery, Gynecology, and Obstetrics* had arrived. Banting was surprised to find a 12-page article by Dr. Moses Barron titled "The Relation of the Islets of Langerhans to Diabetes, with Special Reference to Cases of Pancreatic Lithiasis." The article said that sometimes an autopsy revealed gallstones blocking the pancreatic duct. In these cases, the pancreatic cells that produce digestive juices had disintegrated, but the Langerhans cells all looked normal and healthy, and the patients showed no symptoms of diabetes. Barron also stated that this effect could be recreated in dogs by surgically tying off the pancreatic duct. After several weeks, the entire pancreas shriveled up except for the Langerhans cells. This new information excited Banting to no end.

He went home and anxiously reviewed what he had learned. The Langerhans cells were somehow associated with diabetes; they probably made an unknown hormone X that helped the body burn sugar. Past attempts using pancreatic extracts to relieve diabetic symptoms had been unsuccessful, however. Banting thought perhaps digestive enzymes made by the pancreas had destroyed the unknown hormone during extraction. He needed a method to extract the hormone while protecting it from being digested. If he first tied off the pancreatic duct to destroy the enzyme-making cells and then prepared an extract, perhaps he could obtain active hormone X. At 2:00 A.M. he made a note to himself on a scratch sheet of paper, and the next day he rushed to share his epiphany with Miller.

Miller listened carefully to Banting but then explained that he was a neurophysiologist, and that Banting really should speak with an endocrinologist. He recommended contacting Macleod at the University of Toronto, but Banting knew Macleod was not a believer in the existence of hormone X. He spoke with several other physicians, but they all deferred to Macleod as the leading expert on blood sugar chemistry. Banting hesitantly scheduled an appointment and drove to Toronto.

The meeting with Macleod was very businesslike. Banting nervously shared his ideas, and Macleod politely listened. When pressed about his previous experience, Banting was forced to admit he had no research experience on blood chemistry and very little in other areas. Macleod was not impressed and turned away the discouraged young doctor. Worried his nervousness interfered with his ability to clearly present a strong case for proceeding with the anticipated research, Banting spent that night typing up a written proposal. The next morning, he visited Macleod again, who, this time, agreed to provide Banting with 10 dogs, an assistant proficient in biochemistry, and laboratory space for eight weeks.

After spending several months doing additional library research and working out details of his planned project, Banting moved back to Toronto, leaving behind his private practice and his instructorship at Western University. The assistant Macleod recommended was Charles H. Best, a recent physiology and biochemistry graduate. Like Banting, Best was dedicated and idealistic, but he had previous research experience using chemistry to measure sugar levels in blood and urine.

On May 16, 1921, Banting began surgery on the dogs, tying off the pancreatic ducts in hopes of destroying all the pancreatic tissue except for the islets of Langerhans. The following week, he attempted to remove the pancreas of one dog using a two-step procedure, but the dog developed an infection and died of shock. Using his surgical experience, Banting refined a technique to completely remove the pancreas in one operation. As expected, the dog came down with diabetes. During the six- to eight-week waiting period for the pancreas of the duct-tied dogs to atrophy, Banting named the unknown hormone that they hoped to find "isletin."

The Canadian physiologist Charles Best (1899–1978) codiscovered insulin with Sir Frederick Banting. *(Science Photo Library/Photo Researchers, Inc.)*

On July 6, 1921, the men opened up two dogs whose pancreatic ducts had been tied and were dismayed to find

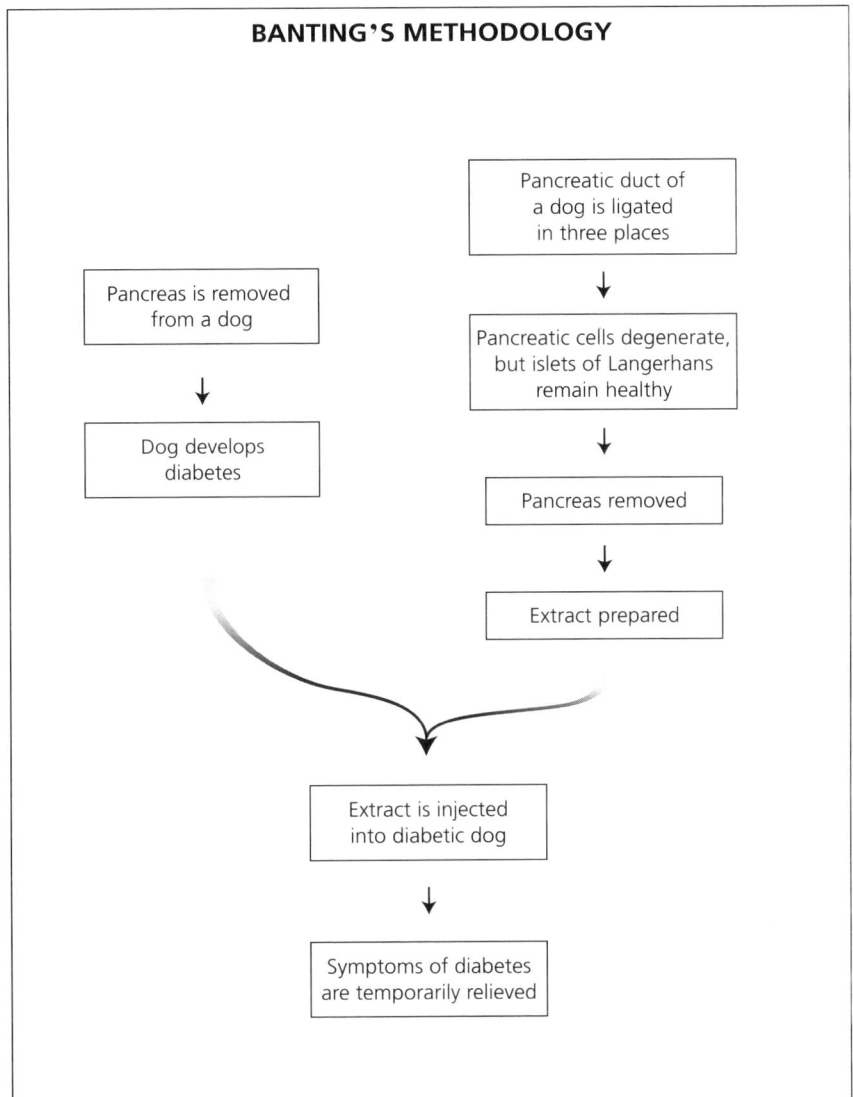

Banting's experience as a surgeon was profoundly useful in carrying out his famous experiments that demonstrated the utility of insulin injections as a treatment for diabetes.

healthy pancreas glands inside. Examination revealed that Banting had tied the ducts too tightly, and new pathways had formed around the ligature. To correct for this, Banting retied the ducts more loosely than before, but in three different places to ensure digestive juices could not flow through them. In a few dogs, degeneration was occurring, but the men decided to let it progress for two more weeks. Banting was worried that they soon would hear from Macleod, who was vacationing in Scotland for the summer. He had originally promised them eight weeks in his lab, and their time was up. They were also broke, so Banting sold his car to buy more dogs.

They removed the pancreas from another dog, which promptly became diabetic. As it approached the coma stage, they cut open a duct-tied dog and removed its degenerated pancreas. The islets of Langerhans still appeared healthy, so they crushed the gland in a chilled, buffered saline solution. After filtration, they injected the extract into the neck vein of the dying dog. In an hour, the dog began to lift its head up. Within a few hours it was sitting up, wagging its tail, and its blood sugar had dropped to almost normal. Within five hours, the urine was completely void of sugar. These were exactly the results Banting and Best had anticipated. A medical miracle had been performed in the sweaty lab under the direction of an inexperienced but ingenious young physician. Isletin successfully treated diabetes.

Unfortunately, the next morning the dog was dead. Isletin was an effective treatment, but it was not a cure. They removed the pancreas from a second dog and waited for it to become ill. Then they made more pancreatic extract from another duct-tied dog, but this time they also made extracts from the liver and spleen to demonstrate that the previous success was due to a substance specifically from the pancreas. When they injected the liver and spleen extracts into the sick dog, nothing happened, but when they injected the pancreatic extract, again, the dog perked up, and within hours the urine contained no sugar. They managed to keep this dog alive for three days.

Though these results pleased Banting, he was disturbed by having to kill healthy animals to obtain extracts that only treated diabetic animals for a short time. He wondered how he could maximize the amount of extract produced and minimize the animals that had to be sacrificed. One technique they tried was exhausting the pancreas by overstimulation with another hormone, but this still yielded limiting amounts.

Macleod returned from vacation, and while he was not overly impressed with their progress, he allowed Banting and Best to continue using his laboratory facilities. Banting was broke once again, however, and worried about the prospect of having to quit because of financial impossibilities. Professor Velyien Henderson, the chair of the pharmacology department, offered Banting a position as a demonstrator for a small salary. His responsibilities were minimal, and the small salary was just enough to allow him to continue his studies.

One day Best came across a paper that said the pancreases of newborns were richer in Langerhans cells than adult pancreases. Since fetuses do not digest their own food in utero, they also would not be producing digestive juices. Banting thought slaughterhouses ought to have a sufficient supply of calf embryos from which they could isolate the pancreases. By noon the following day they had obtained nine embryonic calves from which they extracted isletin. The isletin from calf embryos also reduced the blood sugar levels to normal when given to diabetic dogs. While this method provided more extract than from duct-tied dogs and did not require the sacrifice of otherwise healthy animals, the supply was still limited.

Banting and Best devised a chemical extraction method from adult cattle pancreases involving a combination of acid and alcohol. To ensure it would not cause any undesirable side effects in sick patients, they injected the extract into each other and observed no harmful effects, but of course, neither of them was diabetic. They had a potent extract and were ready for a real human trial.

## A Miracle Cure

The opportunity for a human trial presented itself on January 11, 1922, when a 14-year-old boy was admitted to Toronto General Hospital with a severe case of diabetes. His body had wasted away to a mere 65 pounds (29 kg), and death was imminent. A dose of isletin miraculously reduced the boy's blood sugar! They worked to further purify the extract and optimized the dosage to restore his health.

Now Macleod was amazed at the medical marvel that he had been ignoring until this point. He stopped work on his own

## Biotechnological Insulin Production

Though the procedure developed in 1922 for the extraction and purification of insulin from cattle was successful, it required pancreases from 3 million cattle to supply 100,000 diabetics with insulin for one year. Deep-freezing and transportation of the pancreases were expensive, the process required hazardous chemicals, and physicians worried about the long-term effects. Because the hormone was slightly different in structure to human insulin, some patients developed an allergy to it.

The advent of biotechnology has resulted in an abundant and safe supply of insulin for diabetics worldwide. Microorganisms have been genetically engineered to produce the human insulin protein. In 1978, Herbert Boyer, a researcher from the then new company Genentech, Inc., successfully inserted a fragment of DNA that contained a synthetic gene for human insulin into a *plasmid,* a small piece of circular DNA. The plasmid was introduced into a laboratory strain of the bacteria *Escherichia coli*. Once inside the bacteria, new copies of the gene were synthesized as the bacteria reproduced, and the new bacterial cells also contained the insulin gene. The bacteria produced the protein in large quantities, and the insulin was extracted and purified using biochemical methods. Since then, many additional biopharmaceuticals, such as human growth hormone, factor VIII for hemophilia, somatostatin for acromegaly, and the clot-dissolving agent tissue plasminogen activator, have been produced using bacteria as tiny biological factories.

research and dedicated his entire staff to assisting in the isletin research. He suggested a name change to "insulin," since it was easier to pronounce. A biochemist by the name of Dr. J. B. Collip and a recent graduate named E. C. Noble joined Best in the perfection of a technique called fractional alcoholic precipitation to purify the

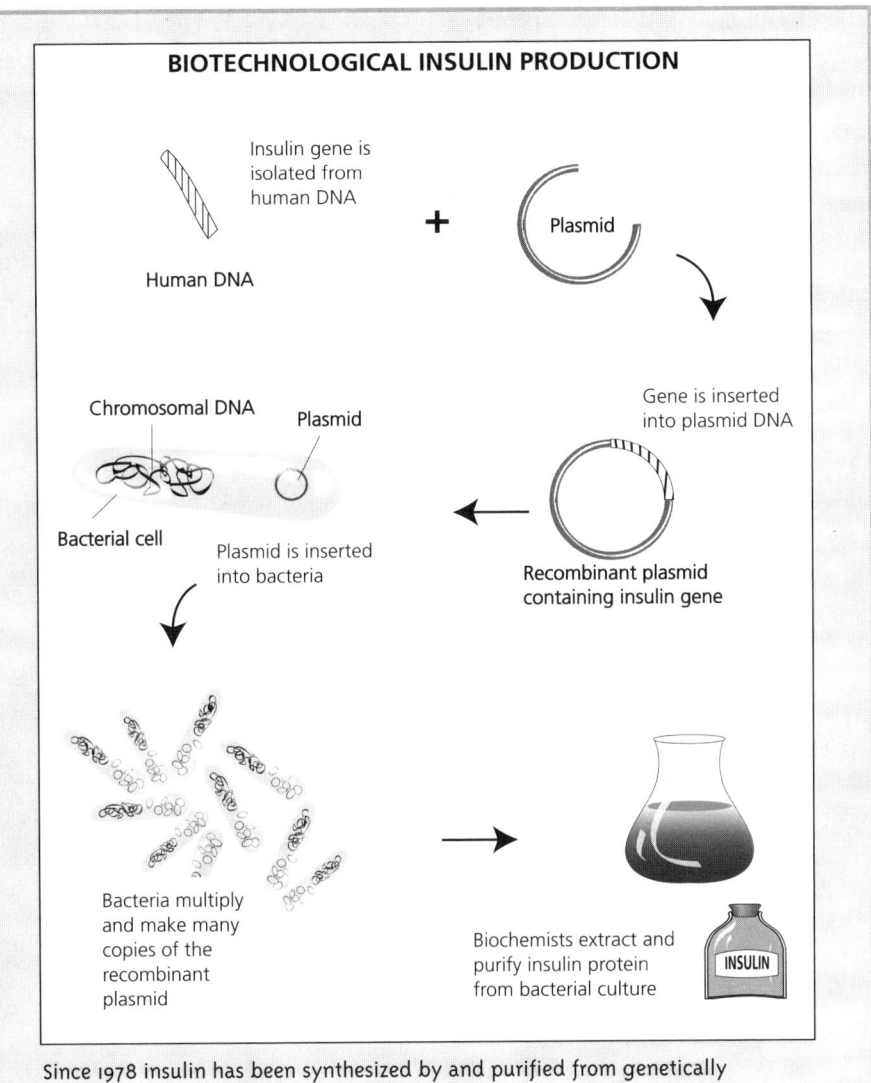

Since 1978 insulin has been synthesized by and purified from genetically modified microorganisms.

insulin from pancreatic extracts. This sort of biochemical research was beyond Banting's expertise.

In February 1923, a former classmate of Banting's from medical school, Joe Gilchrist, came to see Banting. He had developed diabetes during the war and volunteered to act as a human guinea pig for their new extract preparations. Respiration tests showed Gilchrist's body was not burning any sugar. They injected him with insulin, and a few hours later he was producing sugar-free urine. Once, he accidentally overdosed with insulin but recovered after drinking a nearby beaker of glucose solution. A few months later, Banting obtained permission from the Canadian government to use Toronto's Christie Street Hospital for Returned Soldiers to begin clinical trials. Later they expanded their testing to Toronto General Hospital.

The clinical tests taught them that although insulin worked wonders, diet was still an important factor in treatment. They figured out the proper doses of insulin and determined that injections worked best if administered 20 to 30 minutes before a meal. They learned to recognize the signs of insulin overdose and that administration of glucose could prevent insulin shock. Before these tests, six of every 10 diabetics died from coma, and every child was doomed. With the availability of insulin, the death rate dropped considerably.

## Mistaken Credit

Banting and Best published their findings, "The Internal Secretion of the Pancreas," in the November 1921 issue of the *Journal of Laboratory and Clinical Medicine*. Banting publicly announced their results at a medical meeting in New Haven, Connecticut, in late 1922. He was not an experienced or polished speaker, but Macleod, who was chairing the meeting, spoke next. Macleod did a much better job telling the story but failed to emphasize who actually performed the work, thus many believed that Macleod headed the research. The American Association of Physicians in Chicago asked Macleod to come speak. Again, he failed to clarify who led the research that led to the discovery of insulin.

Continued clinical trials gave excellent results, and soon commercial drug companies everywhere were given the instructions on how to produce insulin, but people flocked to Toronto. They wanted to see Banting, the miracle physician, and express their appreciation for saving their lives. Banting was overwhelmed by the gratitude and gifts. He temporarily opened an office to treat diabetics, but he only charged minimal fees to treat his patients.

With Best and Collip, Banting patented the process for insulin production, but not for personal financial gain. He only wanted to ensure that a certain level of quality was maintained. The profits were used to fund future research projects. He received numerous medals, awards, and honorary degrees from several nations. Even the king of England requested an interview with Canada's most famous son. In 1923, Banting was appointed the first full professor of medical research in the history of the University of Toronto. The chair was named the Banting and Best Chair of Medical Research. With the large amount of financial support received as a result of Banting's success, the university planned to open the Banting Research Foundation. The Canadian parliament granted him a lifetime annuity.

The biggest honor bestowed on Banting, however, was the Nobel Prize in physiology or medicine in 1923. The award infuriated Banting, as the recipients were named as Macleod and Banting, a major blunder by the Nobel committee. Banting did not mind sharing the award with anyone but was angered that Best was not also named. Best was the one who sweated with him, shared meals cooked over a Bunsen burner in the lab, and believed in what they were doing. Banting was so upset by this injustice he wanted to refuse the award, but his friends convinced him not to give up the honor for the sake of his nation, Canada. He did send a telegram that was to be read aloud to Dr. Eliot P. Joslin, the chair of a meeting at Harvard Medical School, where Best was speaking to medical students. The telegram publicly acknowledged Best's contribution and pledged half the award money to Banting's faithful colleague. This act motivated Macleod to share his award with Collip. Banting also insisted the order of names be changed to Banting and Macleod.

On June 4, 1925, Banting married Marion Robertson, a radiology technician whom he had met briefly before being discharged from the army. They had one son, William Robertson Banting in 1929. Banting fulfilled the responsibilities of fame, but he was always anxious to return home and spend time with his only son. Though his marriage ended in divorce in 1932, Banting received custody of Bill.

## Silicosis and Wartime Research

After spending so much time touring, lecturing, and treating diabetic patients, Banting was anxious to return to laboratory research. He now had a secretary, a laboratory technician, two graduate students, and his own cramped laboratory. Banting was a good teacher in the lab. He forced his students to think for themselves, taught them to speak simply and to get at the heart of a matter. His research interests included cancer, chemical treatments of mental disorders, and royal jelly (the food of the queen honey bee), but he made the most progress examining silicosis.

The symptoms of silicosis, a lung disease that affected mostly miners, included shortness of breath and a persistent cough, and the disease often resulted in total disability. Banting and his workers identified the cause as inhalation of silicon dioxide, which dissolved in the lungs to form silicic acid. The acid irritated the lining of the lungs and caused hardening, or fibrosis, to occur. Filtering the dust from the air was too cost prohibitive, so the Banting team explored other methods to prevent silicosis. They found that dispersal of a fine dust of aluminum powder into the air successfully prevented the formation of silicic acid in the miner's lungs.

The world continued to bestow new honors and responsibilities on Banting. The University of Toronto opened a new research center, the Banting Research Institute. The formal opening was in 1930, and Banting was the central figure for opening ceremony plans. A few days before the official opening, he suffered an attack of acute appendicitis. Not wanting to disappoint the university officials, he delayed the necessary emergency surgery so he could attend the formal ceremonies. In 1934, he was created a Knight Commander of the Civil Division of the Order of the British Empire. He also served the Canadian government in many capacities. For example, as chairman of the Medical Research Committee of the National Research Council, he surveyed the national medical facilities and recommended the formation of a committee of Aviation Medical Research, which he chaired.

In 1937, he married Henrietta Ball, who worked at the Banting Institute on chemotherapy and tuberculosis research. In 1939, right before Canada declared war, Banting rejoined the army for a second time. He was assigned the rank of major, and the government gave him the task of organizing and administering a major research program. The wartime medical research that he directed included decompression studies, development of an antidote for mustard gas, and the invention of a protective flight suit for airmen.

In February 1941, Banting was flying to England to present the findings on the newly developed flight suits. The plane's engine failed during flight, and Banting died following the crash landing over Newfoundland. The news devastated Canada. Banting lay in state at the University of Toronto's Convocation Hall, where thousands came to pay their last respects. Sir Frederick Banting was given full military honors at his funeral.

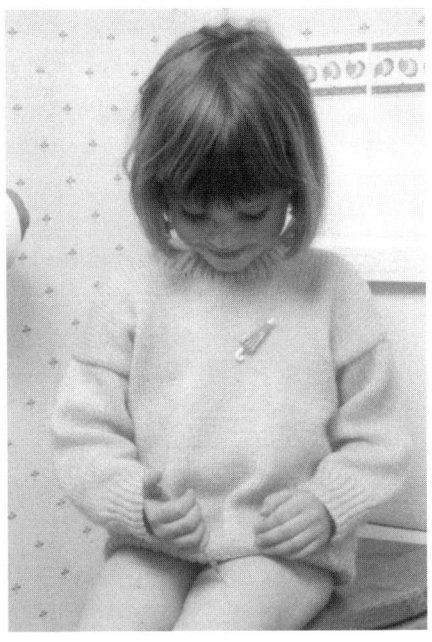

Today diabetic patients are taught to administer their own insulin injections at home, minimizing their dependence upon doctors. *(Chris Priest and Mark Clarke/Science Photo Library/Photo Researchers, Inc.)*

The International Diabetes Federation established the Banting and Best Memorial Lectureship and the American Diabetes Association established the Banting Medal and Memorial Lectureship. The Banting Research Foundation continues to commemorate Banting's discovery of insulin by supporting medical research for young Canadian scientists. The Banting and Best Diabetes Centre at the University of Toronto supports and advances diabetes research, education, and patient care. Despite all these tributes, Banting would be more pleased that, from his efforts, millions of people afflicted with diabetes are living healthy, enjoyable lives. Though experts on sugar metabolism once believed the disease was hopeless, the shy, unpaid medical researcher toiled away in a hot, cramped attic lab to which he had practically to beg to gain access. Sir Frederick Banting and his assistant, Charles Best, maintained hope and, as a result, discovered the miracle hormone insulin.

# CHRONOLOGY

| | |
|---|---|
| 1891 | Frederick Banting is born on November 14 in Alliston, Ontario, in Canada |
| 1910 | Enters Victoria College in Toronto as a theology major |
| 1912 | Registers as a student of medicine at the University of Toronto |
| 1916 | Banting graduates from medical school. He joins the Canadian Army Medical Corps as a lieutenant during World War I and is later promoted to captain |
| 1918 | Receives the Military Cross for his bravery under fire |
| 1919 | Starts working as an orthopedic surgeon at the Hospital for Sick Children in Toronto |
| 1920 | Banting opens a private practice in London, Ontario, and accepts a part-time instructorship at the Western University (now the University of Western Ontario) medical school. He also convinces Macleod to support his research at the University of Toronto |
| 1921 | Banting and Best discover that pancreatic extract injected into a dog lowers its blood sugar levels. They publish their work, "The Internal Secretion of the Pancreas," in the November 1921 issue of the *Journal of Laboratory and Clinical Medicine* |
| 1922 | Insulin injected into a human diabetic lowers blood sugar levels |
| 1923 | Banting and Macleod receive the Nobel Prize in physiology or medicine. Banting shares his prize with Best, and Macleod shares his prize with Collip. Banting is appointed the first full professor of medical research in the history of the University of Toronto |

| 1939 | Rejoins the army as a major |
|---|---|
| 1941 | On February 21, Banting is killed in a plane crash in Newfoundland while on a medical mission |

## FURTHER READING

Bliss, Michael. *The Discovery of Insulin.* Toronto: University of Toronto Press, 2000. Vivid narrative of the medical breakthrough and the personalities involved.

Discoveryofinsulin.com. Available online. URL: http://www.discoveryofinsulin.com. Accessed on March 7, 2005. A fabulous Web site with numerous informative links to biographies of all the relevant personnel and to diabetes organizations.

Gillispie, Charles C., ed. *Dictionary of Scientific Biography.* Vol. 1. New York: Scribner, 1970–76. Good source for facts concerning personal background and scientific accomplishments but assumes reader has basic knowledge of science.

Nobelprize.org. "The Nobel Prize in Physiology or Medicine 1923." Available online. URL: http://www.nobelprize.org/medicine/laureates/1923/index.html. Last modified June 16, 2000. Includes links to biographies and Nobel lectures for both Banting and Macleod.

Stone, Tanya Lee, ed. *Scientists: Their Lives and Works.* Vol. 7. Detroit: U*X*L, 2002. Contains 30 biographies of scientists, including impact boxes. Intended for middle and high school students.

# J. Robert Oppenheimer

## (1904–1967)

J. Robert Oppenheimer was named the father of the atomic bomb for his role in directing the development of atomic weapons. *(Los Alamos National Laboratory/Science Photo Library/Photo Researchers, Inc.)*

## Construction of the First Nuclear Weapon

Pound for pound, the power of a nuclear explosion is 100,000 times more destructive than TNT. When Albert Einstein declared that $E = mc^2$, he provided the world with information that led to the development of such potent nuclear weapons. Einstein determined that the energy of a body equals its mass times the square of the speed of light. Since the value for the speed of light is so great

(186,000 miles, or 300,000 km, per second), and its square is even larger, the amount of energy contained in even the tiniest piece of matter is enormous. Nuclear fission, or the splitting of atomic nuclei, can release this energy. In the 1940s, the United States coordinated a secret research program to construct atomic bombs. The Manhattan Project was headed by a brilliant physicist who is best remembered for his success in leading a team of 1,500 scientists and technicians located at Los Alamos, New Mexico. The bombs they constructed ended World War II and propelled science into an exciting and terrifying new era.

J. Robert Oppenheimer was a pioneer in the field of quantum mechanics, the study of matter and radiation at the atomic level. After quickly mastering quantum theory in Europe, he established one of the first world-class theoretical research centers in the United States. During World War II, Oppenheimer was selected for his innate genius to direct the design and construction of the first atomic bomb. He was an effective, charismatic leader whose contributions during and after the war advanced theoretical physics.

## Born with a Silver Spoon

J. Robert Oppenheimer was born to an affluent New York couple, Julius and Ella Freedman Oppenheimer, on April 22, 1904. His father was an immigrant from Germany who made his fortune in the textile import business, and his mother was a talented painter who taught art. Robert had one younger brother, named Frank, and they grew up comfortably with a maid, a butler, and a chauffeur. The family frequently traveled, and on one trip to Germany Robert's grandfather presented him with a set of rocks, sparking an interest in rock and mineral collecting. At age 11, Robert was elected the youngest member of the New York Mineralogical Society, and he presented his first paper when he was only 12 years old. He was more interested in books than sports, but he did learn to sail the family's two boats.

Robert attended a private school, the Ethical Culture School in New York, and graduated with honors in 1921. He planned to enroll at Harvard University that fall, but a bout with dysentery contracted during a trip to Europe prevented such plans. After a year of recovery, his parents suggested he travel out west with his high school English teacher, Herbert Smith. They visited a ranch in the Pecos River Valley of New Mexico, where Robert learned to ride horses and fell in love with the geography of the region. He returned to this area later in life.

In autumn 1922, Oppenheimer enrolled at Harvard University, where he studied everything from classical literature to mathematics. He majored in chemistry but fell in love with physics. When he was not in the library, Oppenheimer was in the laboratory working with physics professor Percy Bridgman. In only three years, Oppenheimer graduated summa cum laude and went to England to study at the Cavendish Laboratory of Cambridge University. He hoped to work with the Nobel laureate Ernest Rutherford (chemistry, 1908), who had discovered the atomic nucleus, but Rutherford did not feel Oppenheimer was qualified enough. Another Nobel laureate (physics, 1906), Sir Joseph John Thomson, who had discovered the electron in 1897, accepted Oppenheimer into his laboratory. As intelligent as Oppenheimer was, he was clumsy in the laboratory, and his ineptness frustrated him. Being at a world-class research institution, however, he came into contact with several other brilliant physicists. When he was exposed to theoretical physics, he realized he had found his niche.

## Master of the New Physics

Some physicists, called experimentalists, perform experiments to test hypotheses. They then compare the observed results with predictions that are based on theories put forth by theoretical physicists, who use mathematics to explain natural phenomena. Quantum mechanics, based on quantum theory, which helps scientists to understand the behavior of atoms and subatomic particles such as electrons, was just emerging as an exciting new field of physics. The dawn of modern physics brought with it the tools to solve phenomena that were inexplicable by classical methods. When Oppenheimer was invited to work with Max Born, who was crafting the mathematical basis for the new quantum theory at the University of Göttingen, he immediately accepted.

Before arriving in Göttingen in 1926, Oppenheimer had published two papers in the *Proceedings of the Cambridge Philosophical Society*: "On the Quantum Theory of Vibration-Rotation Bands" and "On the Quantum Theory of the Problem of the Two Bodies." The papers demonstrated his command of the new ideas and established Oppenheimer as a gifted theoretical physicist. With Born, he cowrote "Quantum Theory of Molecules," which introduced the Born-Oppenheimer approximation to explain the behavior of molecules using quantum mechanics. The method that they proposed for partitioning the energy of a molecule became standard in quantum physics. Oppenheimer also demonstrated that an electric field could be used to extract electrons from the surface of a metal. The scanning tunneling microscope, which allows scientists to observe atomic scale images of metal surfaces, is based on this discovery. Oppenheimer earned a doctorate in theoretical physics in spring 1927, and from 1928 to 1929 continued performing research on quantum mechanics in Leiden, Holland, and Zurich, Switzerland. Oppenheimer was one of the first to apply quantum mechanics to solve problems that classical physics could not solve. Others recognized and admired his ability to grasp problems quickly and to ask meaningful probing questions.

## Theoretical Physics in the United States

In 1929, Oppenheimer accepted simultaneous assistant professorships at the University of California in Berkeley and the California Institute of Technology (Caltech) in Pasadena. Before his arrival in California, Europe was the core for research in theoretical physics, but Oppenheimer established a world-class theoretical research center at Berkeley. Although he was an unpolished lecturer at first, students and colleagues recognized his underlying brilliance and were willing to ignore his intellectual snobbery to learn from and with him. His students and postdoctoral fellows followed him to and from Berkeley and Pasadena each season. He was known for treating his students to dinner at extravagant restaurants and acquainting them with cultured activities such as chamber music concerts.

Under Oppenheimer's direction, Berkeley scientists focused on problems of relativistic quantum mechanics (quantum mechanical systems where the number of particles can change) and the theory of electromagnetic fields. Research performed by Oppenheimer in 1930 dispelled the belief that protons are the antimatter equivalent of electrons. He essentially predicted the existence of the positron, a positively charged particle with a mass equal to that of a negatively charged electron. In 1932, American physicist Carl David Anderson from Caltech discovered the predicted positron, earning him the Nobel Prize in physics in 1936. In 1939, Oppenheimer predicted the existence of black holes. He discovered a phenomenon called the cascade process, in which cosmic ray particles could break down into another generation of particles. He also advanced research in particle physics (the branch of physics concerned with the behavior and properties of elementary particles) by showing that deuterons (particles made up of a proton and a neutron) could be accelerated to a greater energy than neutrons by themselves, and therefore used to bombard positively charged nuclei at high energies.

During his 13 years at Berkeley, Oppenheimer associated closely with members of the Communist Party. At the time, Russia was an ally of the United States, which was suffering through the Great Depression. Many liberal students and professors sought answers to the nation's problems by embracing ideals shared with communists, such as racial integration, an end to unemployment, and fair pay for employees. Oppenheimer's own brother and sister-in-law were members, as was a woman he seriously dated for three years. The repressive actions of the Russian dictator Joseph Stalin later repulsed Oppenheimer and turned him off to communism, but these associations came back to haunt him later in life.

In 1940, Oppenheimer married Katherine (Kitty) Puening Harrison, who had three previous husbands. They had their first child, a son named Peter, in 1941 and a daughter, Katherine (Toni), in 1944.

# The Controversial Manhattan Project

Physicists began working on the theory of nuclear fission in the 1930s. Nuclear fission is the process of splitting a large nucleus into two smaller nuclei, thus changing the atom of one element into two atoms of different elements. German scientists discovered that the

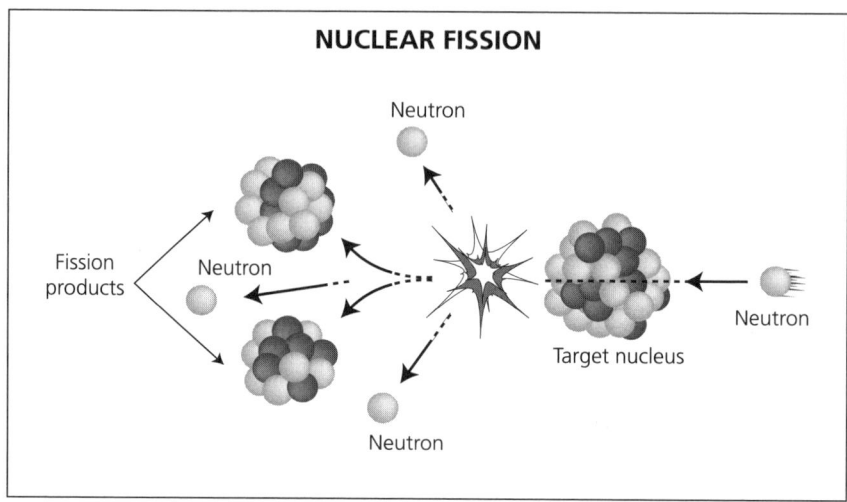

During nuclear fission, an atom is split into two smaller products, and two or three neutrons are released. They can then be captured by a nearby nucleus, initiating a chain reaction. During the process, some of the original mass is converted to energy.

bombardment of a uranium atom (atomic number 92) with a neutron caused it to break into two smaller radioactive nuclei, converting a tiny bit of matter to an enormous amount of released energy. In addition to catalyzing fission, neutrons are also released during nuclear fission. The newly released neutrons bombard other adjacent nuclei, causing them to split, and a chain reaction results. This happens millions of times per second. Scientists realized this phenomenon could be exploited to create an atomic bomb more powerful than any other form of weaponry.

World War II began on September 1, 1939, when Germany invaded Poland, and the United States was drawn into the war when Japanese naval air forces bombed Pearl Harbor on December 7, 1941. American scientists raced to create an atomic bomb, a feat they believed would win the war. The scientists of the Radiation Laboratory at Berkeley decided uranium was the best choice of chemical element to use in a nuclear fission reaction. In theory, the idea was simple—start a chain reaction by hitting a chunk of uranium metal with neutrons—but there were many technical problems that had to be overcome. The director of the Radiation Laboratory, Ernest Lawrence, worked furiously to try to separate uranium-235 from its chemically indistinguishable isotope, uranium-238. Isotopes are atoms of the same chemical element that differ in the amount of matter that they contain. Nuclei of uranium-235 will undergo nuclear fission, and so it was the desired form of the element; unfortunately, it was more than 100 times less abundant in nature. Elsewhere, scientists debated the feasibility of a nuclear reactor and examined other aspects of bomb production, such as how to best initiate the chain reaction and how to assemble the bomb. The lack of a coordinated effort coupled with the necessity for extreme secrecy prevented real progress.

In 1942, the U.S. government organized a collective effort, code-named the Manhattan Project, with the objective of developing an atomic bomb. General Leslie Groves showed tremendous insight when he selected Oppenheimer, who had no previous administrative experience, to direct the project. While Oppenheimer generally was opposed to war, the repulsive Nazi regime forced him to fight back in the only way he knew how—with his brain. Oppenheimer suggested that the goal would be met more easily if the scientists all worked together in one lab, where they could share ideas regularly and communicate freely without worrying about security. Groves agreed. Oppenheimer's first task was to recruit top-notch scientists to work on the secret project and convince them to move to a remote desert plateau in Los Alamos, New Mexico, where they would be housed in a dormitory of a former boys' boarding school. Military forces quickly assembled the makings of a little town to house 1,500 scientists and staff and their 3,000 accompanying family members, all of whom had to pass stringent security clearance testing.

Oppenheimer was an excellent choice for director. He was able to attract the nation's top minds and encourage them to work together toward a common goal. He diffused situations caused by overinflated egos, set up a democratic system of leadership, organized weekly progress discussions and brainstorming sessions for group leaders, and established a regular seminar series for all scientists on staff. Four main divisions were created: experimental

## Enrico Fermi

The Italian physicist Enrico Fermi was a gifted theoretical and experimental physicist. Born in Rome, on September 29, 1901, he was a precocious learner and, at the age of 20, earned a doctorate degree in physics from the University of Pisa. After performing postdoctoral research with Max Born at the University of Göttingen and with the Dutch physicist Paul Ehrenfest at the University of Leiden, he returned to Italy where he became a lecturer in mathematical physics and mechanics at the University of Florence.

Fermi established himself by publishing a paper that applied Pauli's exclusion principle to atoms in a gas. Pauli's exclusion principle states that no two electrons in the same atom can have the same set of quantum numbers. In 1927, Fermi became a professor of theoretical physics at the University of Rome, where he remained until 1938. He proposed the existence of a weak force that caused beta decay, a type of radioactive decay in which a neutron breaks down into a proton and an electron. After Irène and Frédéric Joliot-Curie discovered artificial radioactivity, Fermi figured out a method of using neutrons, rather than alpha particles (positively charged particles composed of two protons and two neutrons), to bombard atomic nuclei in order to create radioactive isotopes. He determined that slow neutrons (low-energy neutrons) worked better than fast neutrons and was able to create radioactive isotopes of 37 different elements using this technique. When he bombarded the element uranium with slow neutrons, he unknowingly accomplished nuclear fis-

physics, theoretical physics, chemistry and metallurgy, and ordnance. Oppenheimer fully comprehended the technical information of each area. The workers described their leader as being omnipresent and having the uncanny ability of being able to enter

sion, in which the atomic nucleus is split, releasing enormous amounts of energy.

In 1938, the Austrian physicist Lise Meitner and her nephew Otto Robert Frisch explained the theory behind nuclear fission. That same year, Fermi was awarded the Nobel Prize in physics for "his demonstrations of the existence of new radioactive elements produced by neutron irradiation, and for his related discovery of nuclear reactions brought about by slow neutrons." Immediately after accepting his award in Stockholm, he escaped the fascist dictatorship of Benito Mussolini by defecting to the United States, where he became a professor of physics at Columbia University and was recruited to participate in the Manhattan Project.

Working at the University of Chicago in 1942, a team of physicists under his leadership successfully accomplished the first sustained nuclear fission reaction. He was surprised to discover that during fission, some of the atomic matter was converted to pure energy. Fermi also determined that passing the neutrons through a material rich in hydrogen would slow them down, increasing the efficiency of their bombardment. In 1944, he moved to Los Alamos, having become a naturalized citizen of the United States, and headed the Manhattan Project's "F" division, which solved special problems as they arose. After the war, Fermi returned to the University of Chicago and became the Charles H. Swift Distinguished Service Professor of Physics. He received many additional medals and awards in recognition of his contributions to physics and the Manhattan Project.

Fermi married Laura Capon in 1928, and they had two children. He died on November 28, 1954, from stomach cancer. Shortly after his death, he was granted the first Enrico Fermi Award from the Atomic Energy Commission. The element fermium, atomic number 100, is named in his honor.

a meeting, immediately grasp what needed to be accomplished, and jump-start the group into moving in the right direction to complete its objectives. He was respected and admired, yet the enormous responsibility he shouldered was taking its toll.

Under intense pressure, his six-foot (1.8-m) frame wasted away to 110 pounds (50 kg). The government pushed for a deadline to test the bomb, which still existed only in the imagination. One pressing practical problem was the lack of an abundant supply of radioactive material for experimentation, forcing the team to rely heavily on theoretical calculations. Factories in Oak Ridge, Tennessee, and Hanover, Washington, were working around the clock to obtain enough fissionable material (uranium and plutonium). The uranium-235 was difficult to purify, and the production of plutonium was lagging.

Another difficulty was figuring out how to control the initiation of the fission reaction that would create the intensely powerful explosion. A condition called critical mass must be achieved, in which the nuclear reactions occurring inside the fissionable material compensate for the neutrons leaving the material. Oppenheimer calculated the critical mass that was necessary to maintain a chain reaction of fission and struggled over how the critical mass should be assembled. To detonate the bomb, two masses containing less than the calculated critical mass had to come together, so that the combined mass would exceed the critical mass. This had to be accomplished extremely rapidly so that the energy released by the initial fission would not propel the masses apart and terminate the chain reaction. One possible method for quickly merging the subcritical masses was the gun assembly prototype, which involved firing a slug of fissionable material into a target mass, like a bullet from a gun. A second method was the implosion method, in which the fissionable material was shaped like a hollow ball encircled by chemical explosives. When the explosives were detonated, the force would instantaneously crush the fissionable material, increasing its density and causing it to reach critical mass. (Critical mass is dependent not only on total mass but also on concentration). The implosion method required evenly distributing the explosives around the core of fissionable material, an engineering task that proved to be extremely difficult. Oppenheimer had scientists working on both methods, and anxiously awaited an optimistic report from either team. The teams determined that the uranium bomb would need to use the simpler but more rugged gun method to initiate the chain reaction, whereas the plutonium bomb would

**FAT MAN BOMB**

The plutonium bomb was named the Fat Man due to its shape. It was 12 feet (3.7 m) high, five feet (1.5 m) wide, and weighed five tons (4,500 kg).

employ the more efficient implosion method. In the end, the Manhattan Project created two plutonium "Fat Man" bombs and one uranium "Little Boy" bomb.

The world's first nuclear weapon was detonated on July 16, 1945, over the Alamogordo desert sands in New Mexico. Observers described the early morning sky as being illuminated more brightly than 1,000 Suns. Words from Hindu scripture came to Oppenheimer's mind, "I am become death, shatterer of worlds." The Los Alamos community was elated for accomplishing a seemingly insurmountable task in such a short period of time. The proud efforts of open collaboration among scientific geniuses under the effective leadership of one of their own were celebrated, though only briefly, as awe was replaced by the terrible reality.

Germany surrendered on May 7, 1945, but sadly, Japan would not. The government asked a committee of four scientists (Oppenheimer, Lawrence, Fermi, and Arthur Compton) for their opinions on the use of an atomic bomb against Japan. Millions had died in the war already, and it was thought a million more would die if the Allies (United States, Soviet Union, United Kingdom, France, and China) proceeded with a military invasion. Based on

**78**  Science, Technology, and Society

Atomic explosion. The mushroom cloud, here shown over New Mexico, came to symbolize the atomic age. *(Los Alamos National Laboratory/Science Photo Library/Photo Researchers, Inc.)*

this assumption, the panel recommended using the bomb. President Harry S. Truman gave the order, and on August 6, 1945, the bomber *Enola Gay* dropped a uranium Little Boy bomb on

Hiroshima, demolishing five square miles (13 km$^2$) in the city's center and ending between 78,000 and 200,000 lives. When Japan stubbornly refused to surrender, on August 9, Fat Man was dropped on Nagasaki, killing 40,000 people. Many more died later from the effects of radiation. Japan surrendered to the Allies on August 14, 1945, ending the war that cost 17 million military deaths and millions more civilian lives from war-related causes. Oppenheimer felt as if he had done something terribly wrong. He admitted to Truman that he felt as if he had blood on his hands and resigned from the project. For his efforts, he received a certificate of gratitude from General Groves and the Presidential Medal of Merit in 1946, and he then returned to teaching at Caltech.

## A Question of Loyalties

During the war, the Soviet Union and the United States grew to become powerful nations. After the war, the amicable union deteriorated, ushering in the cold war. The United States feared that the Soviets would expand communism across the world and became suspicious of anyone with ties to the Communist Party. Oppenheimer became very concerned about potential future uses of atomic weaponry and did what was in his own power to halt the nuclear arms race. As a scientific adviser to the highest levels of government, he helped compose the Acheson-Lilienthal Report that called for stringent international controls on the development of atomic energy to ensure world peace. The plan, which was altered slightly and proposed to the United Nations, was vetoed by the Soviet Union. In 1947, Oppenheimer was appointed the chair of the General Advisory Committee of the Atomic Energy Commission. In this position until 1952, he advocated placing the development of nuclear power in the control of civilians.

Oppenheimer became director of the Institute for Advanced Study at Princeton University in 1947. The Institute was an intellectual think tank, and several prominent scientists including Albert Einstein worked there. Under Oppenheimer's leadership, the reputation of the center as a mecca for theoretical physics research as well as humanities and social science studies escalated; unfortunately, he rarely had time to perform his own research anymore. He was a frequent lecturer on atomic energy controls and the politics of science.

President Truman was pushing for the speedy development of a hydrogen bomb, which is hundreds of times more powerful than the bombs developed under Oppenheimer's leadership. Oppenheimer, whose public opinions largely influenced the minds of Americans, openly opposed developing the hydrogen bomb, angering many top officials. In December 1953, under suspicion of disloyalty, Oppenheimer's security clearance was withdrawn, meaning he no longer had access to any classified information. He chose to withstand a hearing, which more closely resembled a mock trial, to regain his security clearance. He admitted to having relationships with members of the Communist Party during his years at Berkeley, but in those days, the Soviets were allies of the United States and many Americans had communist ties. He had little opportunity to explain his relationships or the reasons for his opposition to the creation of the hydrogen bomb, the circumstances that aroused suspicion of his loyalties. His former ties with members of the Communist Party, interestingly, had been known by the government at the time he was appointed director of the Manhattan Project. Neither Oppenheimer nor his lawyer had access to any of the documentation that was being presented as evidence in his hearing, including memos Oppenheimer himself had written years before. His phones were illegally tapped, and the government had access to his private conversations with his lawyer. The decision to revoke Oppenheimer's security clearance appeared to have been made before the three-week-long hearing even began. Oppenheimer's years of dedication to the nation's military efforts and their success seemed forgotten. In the end, no evidence of sharing information with Soviets was found, but his clearance was revoked in April 1954 based on supposed defects in his character.

Downhearted, Oppenheimer returned to Princeton to serve as director of the Institute of Advanced Study, where he found tremendous support from his colleagues, who were convinced of his loyalty. He continued to lecture frequently and wrote about the relationship between science and culture, including an influential book titled *Science and the Common Understanding*, in 1953. In an act of reconciliation, in 1963, President Lyndon B. Johnson presented

Oppenheimer the Enrico Fermi Award from the Atomic Energy Commission. Though it was not a direct apology from the government, it was a public acknowledgement of the many significant contributions and sacrifices he had made for his country.

In 1966, Oppenheimer was diagnosed with throat cancer, and he retired from the Institute. He died on February 18, 1967, at the age of 62, in Princeton, New Jersey.

Oppenheimer quickly mastered quantum theory and guided a whole generation of young theorists in the new physics. As a researcher, he made significant advances in the field of particle physics and contributed to many other fields. As director for the design and construction of the atomic bomb, he used his talents to create the world's most terrifying weapon and, simultaneously, to end the world's most murderous war. After becoming involved in the Manhattan Project, his personal physics research was diminished, but as a public figure and a scientific consultant to the highest levels of government, he continued to have an enormous influence on physics research and science policy for the remainder of his life.

## CHRONOLOGY

| | |
|---|---|
| 1904 | Robert Oppenheimer is born on April 22 in New York, New York |
| 1925 | Receives a bachelor's degree from Harvard University and begins working with Sir J. J. Thomson at Cambridge University |
| 1926 | Oppenheimer publishes two papers in the *Proceedings of the Cambridge Philosophical Society,* "On the Quantum Theory of Vibration-Rotation Bands" and "On the Quantum Theory of the Problem of the Two Bodies." He moves to the University of Göttingen to complete his doctoral dissertation working under Max Born |
| 1927 | Publishes "Quantum Theory of Molecules" with Born and receives his doctorate degree in theoretical physics from the University of Göttingen |

| | |
|---|---|
| 1928–29 | Pursues postdoctoral research in Leiden, Holland, and Zurich, Switzerland |
| 1929–42 | Oppenheimer researches and teaches at both Caltech and the University of California at Berkeley, where he establishes a world-class theoretical research center. He performs research in areas ranging from particle physics to cosmic rays |
| 1942 | General Leslie Groves selects Oppenheimer to direct the U.S. Manhattan Project to build atomic weaponry |
| 1945 | Oppenheimer's team successfully tests a plutonium bomb in Alamogordo, New Mexico, in July. In August, the United States drops bombs on Hiroshima and Nagasaki, ending World War II. Oppenheimer returns to Caltech to teach |
| 1946 | Receives the Presidential Medal of Merit for contributions to the war effort |
| 1947 | Is named director of the Institute of Advanced Study at Princeton University and is appointed chair of the General Advisory Committee of the U.S. Atomic Energy Commission |
| 1953 | Security clearance for Oppenheimer is withdrawn based on suspicion of disloyalty. Oppenheimer publishes a book, *Science and the Common Understanding* |
| 1954 | A security hearing fails to clear Oppenheimer of the charges against him. He is dismissed from government service |
| 1963 | President Lyndon B. Johnson presents Oppenheimer with the Enrico Fermi Award for outstanding contributions to physics from the Atomic Energy Commission |
| 1966 | Retires from the Institute of Advanced Study |
| 1967 | Dies from throat cancer on February 18 in Princeton, New Jersey |

# FURTHER READING

*Biographical Memoirs. National Academy of Sciences.* Vol. 71. Washington, D.C.: National Academy of Sciences, 1997.

Memoir of Oppenheimer's life and accomplishments written by a distinguished colleague.

Fox, Karen. *The Chain Reaction: Pioneers of Nuclear Science.* New York: Franklin Watts, 1998. The story of nuclear science from the discovery of radioactivity to the understanding of nuclear power and the harnessing of nuclear energy.

Herken, Gregg. *Brotherhood of the Bomb: The Tangled Lives and Loyalties of Robert Oppenheimer, Ernest Lawrence, and Edward Teller.* New York: Henry Holt, 2002. Story of the men involved in founding the nuclear age. Focuses less on science and more on the personalities and politics involved.

Rummel, Jack. *Robert Oppenheimer: Dark Prince.* New York: Facts On File, 1992. Chronicles the life of Oppenheimer and his involvement in the Manhattan Project. Written for middle and high school students.

*Scientists and Inventors.* New York: Macmillan Library Reference, 1998. Brief profiles of the lives and work of more than 100 notable scientists. Written for middle and high school students.

Smith, Alice Kimball, and Charles Weiner, eds. *Robert Oppenheimer, Letters and Recollections.* Stanford, Calif.: Stanford University Press, 1995. A collection of letters written by Oppenheimer and memories recorded by his colleagues.

# Rachel Carson

(1907–1964)

Rachel Carson is credited for launching the environmental movement by writing *Silent Spring,* a book that revealed the truth about the dangers of pesticide overuse. *(Erich Hartmann, Magnum Photos)*

## The Dangers of Pesticide Overuse

In 1854, Henry David Thoreau wrote the book *Walden*, touching the world with his eloquent evocation of natural harmony, depicting human beings as only a part of the living world. A decade later Ernst Haeckel coined the word *ecology*, and then Ellen Swallow Richards established ecology, the study of the relationships of organisms with one another and to their environment, as a new branch of science. John Muir expressed his outrage at the careless destruction of 2,000-year-old forests by loggers and formed the Sierra Club to preserve the forests of the Sierra Nevada Mountains in 1892. During the first half of the 1900s, Aldo Leopold published numerous articles, pleading with the world to maintain the natural balance and diversity of the Earth's *ecosystems*. All these spokespersons for the protection of the environment set the stage for the environmental movement that was launched by a shy but courageous woman named Rachel Carson. An eminent marine biologist and writer, Carson wrote four books, including one of the most influential books of all time, *Silent Spring*, that warned readers about the irreversible damage caused by the indiscriminate use of *pesticides*. Carson had a talent for making scientific information accessible to general readers, and her book educated and alarmed the public into action.

## An Emerging Author

Rachel Louise Carson was born on May 27, 1907, in Springdale, Pennsylvania. Her father, Robert Warden Carson, was a real estate and insurance salesperson and also worked at the local utility company. Her mother, Maria Frazier McLean Carson, was a former schoolteacher. The Carsons instilled a love of nature into all their children. They lived on a 65-acre farm, and Rachel and her older brother and sister spent their childhoods listening to the songbirds, strolling through the apple orchard, and exploring nature. Rachel attended the local school but did not have many childhood friends. She spent most of her free time reading or with her mother, with whom she shared an especially close relationship throughout her life.

Rachel read everything, but she especially enjoyed reading books about nature and animals by writers such as Ernest Thompson Seton and Henry Williamson. In 1918, she submitted a story to *St. Nicholas*, a literary magazine that published works of young authors. The story, "A Battle in the Clouds," told of a young pilot's struggle after being shot by German gunfire. It was accepted, as were two others over the next year. Though at the time most children only attended public school until the 10th grade, Rachel's parents agreed that she should continue her schooling, so they enrolled her at Parnassus High School, just across the Allegheny River. After graduation in 1925, Rachel enrolled at the Pennsylvania College for Women (PCW, now Chatham College). Because she enjoyed writing, she decided to major in English.

Her father had bought the farm as an investment, with hopes of selling off tracts of land at a profit, but chemical factories built on either side had diminished the value of the land. Her mother did what she could to earn extra money, such as selling eggs from their chickens and fruit from their trees and teaching piano to neighbors, but paying for college was still a struggle. Even though Rachel received some aid in the form of a scholarship, the family had to sell their heirloom china to pay tuition. After an initial adjustment period to being away from home, she participated in such extracurricular activities as basketball, field hockey, the student newspaper, and the literary magazine. During the summertime, Rachel tutored students to earn money.

## Studies of Life

Though she was an English major, in order to fulfill general education requirements, as a sophomore Rachel enrolled in a biology course that changed her life. Learning about nature and the plants and animals she admired and that had brought her pleasure since childhood captivated her. After taking several more biology courses, Rachel changed her major to biology and graduated with high honors in 1929.

Carson spent the summer following graduation as an intern at the Marine Biological Laboratory at Woods Hole, Massachusetts, where she saw the sea for the first time. Examining tissue specimens from ocean organisms under the microscope and studying the nervous system of turtles, she yearned to learn more about marine biology. That fall she entered Johns Hopkins University on a full tuition scholarship to study marine *zoology*. Suffering effects from the Great Depression, her family gave up the farm and moved to Maryland to live with Carson. To help support her family, Carson worked as a laboratory assistant and taught a lower-level zoology course at Johns Hopkins and other courses at the University of Maryland in College Park, all the while working on her master's thesis, titled "The Development of the Pronephros during the

Embryonic and Early Larval Life of the Catfish." The pronephros is a temporary kidney that only functions in catfish embryos for 11 days before being replaced by a permanent kidney. After obtaining a master's degree in zoology in 1932, she continued teaching at Johns Hopkins and the University of Maryland. She began the doctoral program at Johns Hopkins, but in 1935 her father died, leaving her financially obligated to her mother.

# Merger of Two Loves: Science and Writing

Carson contacted Elmer Higgins, whom she had met at Woods Hole in 1929. He was the head of the division of scientific inquiry at the Bureau of Fisheries in Washington, D.C., and in charge of writing a series of radio scripts for a program called *Romance under the Waters*. He invited Carson to help him with this task, and her entertaining and informative scripts exceeded his expectations. In 1936, she took the civil service test required of all government employees, and after obtaining the highest score, she was hired by the bureau as a junior aquatic biologist. When the radio broadcasts were to be published as a booklet, Carson's boss asked her to compose a general introduction. She did, but her boss felt it was too literary for the government booklet, and he suggested she submit it to the magazine *The Atlantic Monthly*. After rewriting the introduction, she eventually submitted her piece, "Undersea," which was accepted for publication. She enjoyed writing very much, and upon receiving such positive feedback, she began writing natural-history articles for the *Baltimore Sunday Sun Magazine*.

Upon reading "Undersea," an editor at the Simon and Schuster publishing company invited Carson to expand her article into an entire book about the ocean and marine life. Carson loved biology and she loved writing. The idea of not having to choose between two exclusive careers thrilled her. Though still working at the bureau, she accepted the proposal and went to work.

Carson was a perfectionist, which made writing *Under the Sea-Wind* a major task. She wanted to instruct her readers about sea life and keep them interested, so she wrote from the animals' perspective. She researched, wrote, and rewrote, carefully choosing every word. The book was divided into three parts: life on the shore, life in the open sea, and life at the sea bottom. Though the book was nonfiction, she wrote it as a story about seabirds and marine animals, naming them (based on their scientific names) and giving them human characteristics. She described their habits and daily activities: a pair of sanderlings named Silverbar and Blackfoot sought sand bugs and crabs in between waves rolling onto the shore, a mackerel named Scomber escaped prey and haul nets, and an eel named Anguilla journeyed out to sea. Her efforts were rewarded when the book was published in 1941, and reviewers praised her ability to make science understandable for the average reader. The timing of the book's release was unfortunate, however, because Japan attacked Pearl Harbor in December, and the United States entered World War II. People were too preoccupied to read a fantastical book about sea life.

Carson was discouraged. She felt that writing books was not worth the time it took. She now was supporting her mother and her two nieces since her sister had died, and was dealing with her own health problems, including appendicitis and shingles. In 1940, the Bureau of Fisheries had merged with the U.S. Biological Survey to form the U.S. Fish and Wildlife Service (FWS). At work Carson contributed to the war effort by writing *conservation* bulletins to educate people about fish and encouraging them to consume fish as an alternative source of protein in times of scarcity. She also continued submitting brief nature articles to popular magazines. By 1949, Carson was promoted to chief editor for all the FWS publications, and she moved to Silver Spring, Maryland, her home base for the remainder of her life.

## Greater Success

Though she remembered the feeling of frustration from the poor sales of her first book, after working on a series of FWS pamphlets, *Conservation in Action*, about the nation's wildlife refuges, she found herself yearning to write another book, a biography of the ocean for the average reader. She was awarded a Eugene F. Saxton Memorial Fellowship so she could afford to take time off from her job at the

FWS to immerse herself fully in her research. She started interviewing oceanographers, reading technical papers, and converting the scientific jargon into understandable prose.

Her goal was to depict the wonders of the ocean while melding the fields of marine biology and physical oceanography. She began by summarizing the origin of the Earth and its oceans and progressed into the history of the ancient Earth and the emergence of the first life forms. She profiled the field of marine geology, described the seasonal changes in the sea, and outlined the divisions of life within the different oceanic zones. The book contained a simplified summary of relatively new information regarding tides, waves, and currents that was gathered during the war. The text emphasized the importance of all life forms in the oceans, from the microscopic protozoa to the larger fish, introducing to readers ecology, the concept of *food chains*, and the interdependence of organisms within a biological community. She also pointed out the potential economic wealth in the forms of minerals and petroleum found within the sea. In a sense, by showing why all nature was worth preserving, she was priming her readers for the acceptance of the ideas she would later propose in her masterpiece, *Silent Spring*.

*The Yale Review*, *Science Digest*, *Nature*, and *The New Yorker* all published portions of her manuscript before it was released. *The Sea Around Us* was published in 1951, jumped onto *The New York Times* best-seller list within two weeks, and remained there for a record 86 weeks. (It was number one for 39 weeks.) This instantly successful book received the National Book Award for nonfiction in 1952 and was voted Outstanding Book of the Year in *The New York Times* Christmas Poll. Carson received the John Burroughs Medal for writing a natural-history book of outstanding literary quality. PCW and Oberlin College awarded Carson honorary doctorate degrees, and the National Academy of Arts and Letters elected her to membership. *Under the Sea-Wind* was rereleased and hit the best-seller list this time. Royalties from both her books permitted her to resign from her government job in 1952 so she could concentrate on writing full-time. She bought land in West Southport, Maine, and built a summer cottage with a breathtaking view of the ocean. There she spent summers with her mother and nieces, wading in the waters looking for marine life.

Having published a book that explored the lives of sea creatures and another on the physical aspects of the oceans, she began toying with the idea of writing a field guide for animals that lived on the Atlantic shores of America. She had applied for and received a fellowship from the Guggenheim Foundation so she could take time off again from FWS, but ended up returning a portion of the money, since sales of her other books now allowed her to quit her job. She struggled for a few years on how to arrange the manual and finally decided to organize it by ecosystem. One section was devoted to life on the rocky shores of New England, another to life on the sandy beaches of the mid-Atlantic, and the third section to life in the coral reefs and mangroves of the south. Titled *The Edge of the Sea* and published in 1955, her third book was also a best seller. The National Council of Women of the United States named it Outstanding Book of the Year, and the American Association for University Women gave Carson an Achievement Award.

The following year, Carson wrote an article providing suggestions for how to teach children to appreciate nature. The article, "Help Your Child to Wonder," was published in *Woman's Home Companion* (1956). This text was adapted into a book, *The Sense of Wonder*, published in 1965 after Carson's death.

## Threat of a Silent Spring

Though Carson never married, she developed several close relationships with women from whom she received support, encouragement, and advice. Much of her correspondence with these women is preserved. One friend, Olga Owens Huckins, mailed Carson a copy of a letter to the editor of the *Boston Herald* complaining about the mosquito control program in Massachusetts. She wrote that in her backyard bird sanctuary, she had discovered as many as 14 lifeless songbirds that she believed died from pesticide spraying. The lifeless birds had their claws clutched to their chests and their bills gaping open as if they died in agony. Carson viewed this dreadful scenario as a call for action.

For more than a decade, companies had been synthesizing a chemical called *dichlorodiphenyltrichloroethane*, a chlorinated hydrocarbon more commonly known as DDT. The Swiss chemist Paul Hermann

**DICHLORODIPHENYLTRICHLOROETHANE**

$$Cl-\underset{}{\bigcirc}-CH(CCl_3)-\underset{}{\bigcirc}-Cl$$

Approximately 1.35 billion pounds (600 million kg) of dichlorodiphenyltrichloroethane, more commonly known as DDT, were used in the United States over a period of three decades before it was banned in 1972.

Müller was awarded the Nobel Prize in physiology or medicine in 1948 for his discovery of DDT as a contact poison against insects. DDT was found to be effective against many types of annoying insect pests, including flies, lice, gnats, beetles, and mosquitoes. After studies showed it was safe for human use at insecticidal doses, it was used to combat typhus and malaria during World War II by killing the insects that transmitted the diseases. At the time, people said Müller was lucky to have discovered a substance so beneficial to medicine while researching it as an insecticide for moths. Slowly, however, scientific reports began to find its use was not as safe as initially believed. Carson had been following these reports since the 1940s, when she first encountered them while working at the FWS.

The American Association of Economic Entomologists published an article concerning DDT's potentially damaging side effects in 1944. The article pointed out that not only were pests killed, but insects that were beneficial to mankind were also killed. For example, insects that fed on crop-destroying pests were killed, as were insects that played an important role in plant pollination. Carson dug into the scientific literature and explored the effects on her own, learning that many fertilized bird eggs never developed or hatched and others hatched malformed animals. The bird population was steadily declining, and Carson believed this was due to the spraying of DDT. She searched for a magazine willing to publish an article about the dangers of DDT, but despite the fact that Carson was a best-selling author, the magazines were all too afraid to publish something so controversial.

Carson decided to write another book, one that pointed out the dangers of this chemical that industries were hailing as the miracle solution to all pests. In a letter to her editor at Houghton Mifflin, she pledged to expose the dangers of supposedly safe pesticides and to provide substantial scientific evidence. This job would require familiarity with the scientific method and scientific literature, and knowledge of cell biology, physiology, ecology, agronomy, organic chemistry, and biochemistry. Though she was recognized as a writer, she was trained as a scientist. Carson convinced her editor that she was up to this task, and she began accumulating evidence.

At first the government and scientific establishment readily supplied Carson with requests for information. After her reason for gathering the evidence became known, however, her requests were often blocked or left unanswered. She examined congressional testimony and interviewed countless medical and agricultural experts. Her motivation was fueled in 1957, when residents of Long Island lost a suit against the state of New York to stop the spraying of DDT for gypsy moths.

Her book, *Silent Spring*, opened with an imaginary scenario of a picture-perfect town in middle America. Suddenly, the farm animals became sick, crops suffered, and birds and chirping insects were no longer heard, all as a result of pesticide and chemical fertilizer overuse. She exposed the truth about the poisonous effects of lingering pesticides and *herbicides* (chemicals that kill weeds) in the soil and water. Carson did not deny the major benefit of pesticide use in agriculture—namely, the increase in crop yield and therefore an increased food supply. She simply asked, "At what cost?" She wanted the use of most pesticides to be evaluated carefully and controlled accordingly, but she passionately believed that DDT needed to be banned altogether. Carson squashed the argument that chemicals lingering in the soil do not directly affect humans by explaining that the dangerous chemicals accumulated in all creatures, beginning with the tiny organisms at the bottom of the food chain, such as *plankton* and small fish, and working their way up to humans. After entering the food chain, the DDT, which cannot dissolve in water, accumulated in the fatty tissues. Those organisms at the top of the food chain were at the greatest risk, since the organisms they ate contained increasingly concentrated amounts of the stored residues, and as a result, they could develop cancer and have shortened life expectancies. Birds were particularly susceptible;

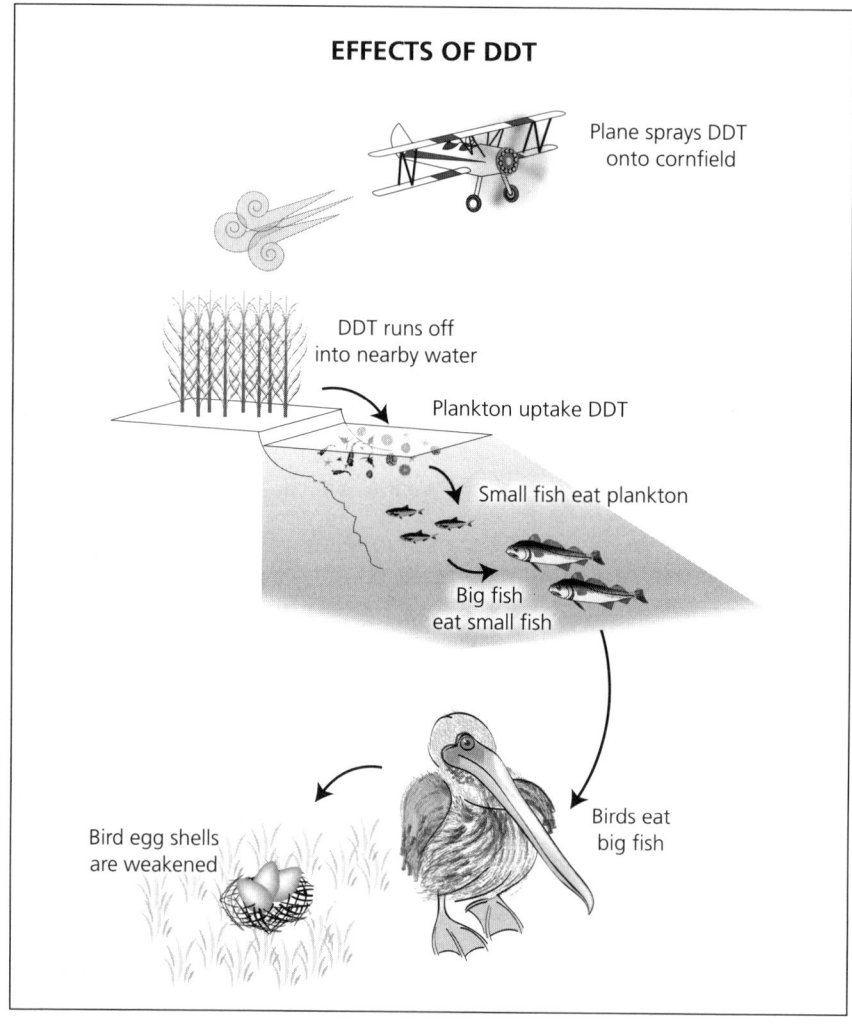

As poisonous pollutants such as DDT travel up the food chain, their concentration effectively increases and can cause irreversible damage.

DDT interferes with their calcium levels, leading to weakened eggshells. Man, as an integral part of the Earth's ecosystem, was not immune. Carson demonstrated DDT toxicity to living cells and said that DDT spraying programs were pointless because the insects developed resistance. None of this information was brand new, but all the previous reports were hidden in scientific journals and focused on one small aspect of the problem. She made this information accessible and meaningful by presenting a clear, complete overview in plain language.

Not only were the reports Carson uncovered appalling, the years she spent performing her extensive research were difficult personally. Her mother and her niece had both passed away, and at the age of 50, she adopted her five-year-old grandnephew, who required more attention than Carson's work permitted. In addition, she was diagnosed with breast cancer and was undergoing radiation treatment. In January 1962, she finally submitted the manuscript for *Silent Spring* to Houghton Mifflin, complete with 55 pages of references supporting her claims.

## Negative Reaction—Positive Change

*Silent Spring* reached number one on the best-seller list within two weeks. The release of her critical book infuriated the billion-dollar chemical and agricultural industries, which were at risk of losing money. Unable to retaliate by discounting the overwhelming scientific evidence presented against pesticide use, they resorted to personal attacks, calling Carson a hysterical woman and assaulting her credentials. But the public bought her book, read it, and took her message to heart. They wrote to their elected representatives in Congress and to government agencies in protest. President John F. Kennedy set up a special panel of the President's Science Advisory Committee to evaluate the positive and negative effects of pesticide use. By May 1963, Rachel Carson was vindicated. She testified to Congress, imploring them to develop new policies to protect the environment. The committee recommended eliminating the use of persistent toxic pesticides. As a result of Carson educating the public and the government on this scientific matter, within one year, more than 40 bills were passed through state legislatures regulating

> ## The Environmental Protection Agency
>
> In response to the public demand for a healthier and cleaner environment, stimulated by Rachel Carson's writing of *Silent Spring*, which educated people about a pressing environmental issue of the 1960s, President Richard M. Nixon proposed and Congress approved the formation of the Environmental Protection Agency (EPA) in 1970. The EPA consolidated several preexisting programs coordinated by the Department of the Interior, the Department of Health, Education, and Warfare, the Department of Agriculture, the Federal Radiation Council, and the President's Council on Environmental Quality. Rachel Carson had proposed the consolidation of all the preexisting programs, believing it would be more efficient to have one agency regulating all environmental issues. The self-reported mission of the EPA is to protect human health and to safeguard the natural environment (air, water, and land) upon which life depends.
>
> The EPA employs more than 18,000 people involved in all aspects of environmental science research, education, and assessment. They

the use of pesticides. Within 10 years, the federal government followed suit. The effects of her discoveries reverberated worldwide. In 1972, the use of DDT was banned in the United States.

# Pioneer of the Environmental and Ecological Movements

Rachel Carson succumbed to cancer on April 14, 1964, in Silver Spring, Maryland. She had received numerous awards and recognition before her passing, including the Conservationist of the Year Award from the National Wildlife Federation, the National Audubon Society Medal, and the Schweitzer Medal of the Animal

develop and enforce regulations, provide financial support for state environmental programs, perform environmental research, sponsor voluntary partnerships and programs, and educate the public to inspire personal responsibility for the environment. More than one dozen major laws form the legal basis for the EPA's programs. Since 1947, the Federal Insecticide, Fungicide, and Rodenticide Act (FIFRA) has regulated the distribution, use, and sale of pesticides. The Federal Pesticide Control Act was passed as an amendment to FIFRA in 1972. Under this legislation, companies are required to register and obtain approval before marketing or distributing pesticides. In order to gain approval, they must prove and document the safety of the product with regard to human and environmental health.

While the EPA's efforts to reduce pollution have been effective, not everyone is thrilled by their existence. It is an extremely expensive enterprise; the proposed 2005 fiscal year's budget is $7.8 billion. Further expenses are incurred by industries complying with the regulations that constrain their operations. Unfortunately, environmental policy is often dictated by legal decisions rather than EPA directives. In addition, companies often exploit the EPA and its regulations to fight against one another.

Welfare Institute. In 1969, the Department of the Interior changed the name of the Coastal Maine Refuge to the Rachel Carson National Wildlife Refu ge. In 1980, she was posthumously awarded the Presidential Medal of Freedom by President Jimmy Carter. Her most satisfying reward was having saved countless voiceless animals, and in turn having benefited humankind.

Not only did Rachel Carson educate the general public regarding marine science and affect change in the way pesticides were used, but she also pioneered movements in environmental conservation and ecology. Ecology is the study of the relationships between organisms and the environment; both affect each other, and ecologists aim to understand how. One avenue of investigation for modern ecologists is a direct consequence of Carson's speculation of the effect of human activities on the environment. Though her content was scientific, Carson's poetic style of writing appealed to general audiences, making it an effective means to educate the public about technical matters. She called attention to the irony that, though the goal of pesticide use was the benefit of mankind, it actually harmed biological communities, including humans. Although the idea of conservation had been around for almost a century, the public as a whole did not take action to preserve nature until Carson revealed and explained how current practices caused contamination of the food supply with substances that caused cancer, genetic damage, and could lead to the extinction of species. She scared the world into caring.

In 1965, friends of Carson founded the nonprofit organization the Rachel Carson Council, to educate the public about chemical contaminants and alternatives. On April 22, 1970, Americans celebrated the first Earth Day, now recognized annually as a means to protest practices damaging to the Earth and to contribute positively to protecting our environment.

## CHRONOLOGY

| | |
|---|---|
| 1907 | Rachel Carson is born on May 27 in Springdale, Pennsylvania |
| 1918 | Publishes "A Battle in the Clouds," in *St. Nicholas* magazine, soon followed by two other stories |
| 1929 | Graduates magna cum laude with a bachelor's degree in science from the Pennsylvania College for Women (now Chatham College). Is awarded an internship at Woods Hole Marine Biological Laboratory at Cape Cod for the summer and a tuition scholarship for graduate study in zoology at Johns Hopkins University |
| 1932 | Receives a master's degree in zoology from Johns Hopkins University |
| 1935 | Starts writing radio scripts for the U.S. Bureau of Fisheries |
| 1936 | Becomes a junior aquatic biologist at the U.S. Bureau of Fisheries |

| | |
|---|---|
| 1937 | Publishes "Undersea" in *The Atlantic Monthly* |
| 1941 | Publishes her first book, *Under the Sea-Wind*, which receives favorable reviews but sells poorly due to the United States' involvement in World War II |
| 1942 | Becomes assistant to the chief of the office of information at the FWS |
| 1943–45 | Writes and edits a series of pamphlets promoting the consumption of fish for wartime conservation of resources |
| 1949 | FWS appoints Carson editor in chief for all publications |
| 1951 | Publishes *The Sea Around Us* and wins numerous literary awards. *Under the Sea-Wind* is republished and also hits the best-seller list. She resigns from her government job |
| 1955 | Publishes *The Edge of the Sea* |
| 1956 | Writes "Help Your Child Wonder" for *Woman's Home Companion*, which was later developed into the book *The Sense of Wonder*, published in 1965 |
| 1962 | Publishes *Silent Spring*. The chemical industry mounts a vicious personal and scientific attack against Carson. Within one year, more than 40 bills are passed in state legislatures to regulate pesticide use |
| 1963 | The president's Science Advisory Committee validates Carson's claims about the dangers of DDT |
| 1964 | Dies on April 14 from breast cancer and heart disease in Silver Spring, Maryland |
| 1980 | Is awarded the Presidential Medal of Freedom—the highest civilian award of the government—posthumously |

## FURTHER READING

Byrnes, Patricia. *Environmental Pioneers*. Minneapolis, Minn.: Oliver Press, 1998. Excellent reference about the lives and work of eight individuals who initiated the modern environmental movement. Written for young adults.

Carson, Rachel. *Silent Spring.* Boston: Houghton Mifflin, 1962. The infamous book that launched the environmental movement.

Garraty, John A., and Mark C. Carnes, eds. *American National Biography.* Vol. 4. New York: Oxford University Press, 1999. Brief accounts of the lives and work of famous Americans in encyclopedia format.

Lear, Linda. *Rachel Carson: Witness for Nature.* New York: Henry Holt, 1997. Full-length, detailed biography written for adult readers.

"The Learning Place Biography Center: Rachel Carson." National Women's History Project, 2003. Available online. URL: http://www.nwhp.org/tlp/biographies/carson/carson-bio.html. Accessed on March 8, 2005. Great resource containing short biographical profile plus links to additional resources.

RachelCarson.org home page. Available online. URL: http://www.rachelcarson.org. Accessed on March 8, 2005. A Web site devoted to the life and legacy of Rachel Carson. Contains several links to a biography, books about Carson, her obituary, and other resources.

Stewart, Melissa. *Rachel Carson: Biologist and Writer.* Chicago: Ferguson Publishing Company, 2001. Emphasizes the development of Carson's career.

# William Shockley

(1910–1989)

William Shockley invented the transistor, initiating a revolution in electronics. (© *The Nobel Foundation*)

## Inventor of the Transistor

A jogger wearing a Walkman is a common site. He can enjoy his music despite the jostling, and if he drops the Walkman, it will usually still work. In the early 1900s, the radio employed bulky, fragile *vacuum tubes*, as did early computers. Today people can carry personal computers in the palm of their hand; it is amazing to think that 50 years ago, a computer capable of performing similar tasks would have occupied an entire building. These incredible advances are possible due to the invention of the *transistor* by a team of scientists led by the American physicist William Shockley in the 1950s. Transistors can amplify electrical signals and act as electronic switches to turn a current on or off. Because they contain no moving parts, they are more durable than vacuum tubes and work faster than a mechanical switch.

## Specialization in Solid-State Physics

William Bradford Shockley was born on February 13, 1910, while his American parents were living in London, England. His father, William Hillman Shockley, was a mining engineer, and his mother, May Bradford Shockley, was a mineral surveyor. The family returned to the United States when William was three years old. They lived in Palo Alto, California, and his mother home-schooled him until he was eight years old. A neighbor who was a professor of physics at Stanford University helped encourage William's early interest in physics. As a teenager, William attended the Palo Alto Military Academy and the Los Angeles Coaching School, where he studied physics. He graduated from Hollywood High School in 1927. He attended the University of California in Los Angeles for one year and then transferred to the California Institute of Technology, earning a bachelor's degree in physics in 1932.

In 1933, Shockley married Jean Alberta Bailey, with whom he had two sons and one daughter. They lived in Cambridge, where Shockley obtained a teaching fellowship and performed research in solid-state physics at the Massachusetts Institute of Technology. Solid-state physics seeks to explain the internal atomic structure and the electronic properties of materials such as metals and plastics. He received a Ph.D. in physics in 1936 with a dissertation titled "Calculation of Wave Functions for Electrons in Sodium Chloride Crystals." This background in solid-state physics prepared Shockley for his first job.

## The Old Technology

Bell Telephone Laboratories, in Murray Hill, New Jersey, offered Shockley a position exploring improvements in communications mechanisms. At the time, vacuum tubes were used to amplify signals in many electronic devices. Vacuum tubes consisted of a glass outer shell from which all the air had been removed and at least two electrodes inside the bulb that were connected to outside electrical circuits. The positively charged electrode (*anode*) was called the collector, and the negatively charged electrode (*cathode*) was called the emitter. When the vacuum tube was connected to a current from an outside source such as a battery, electrons left the emitter. A wire mesh grid between the collector and emitter controlled the strength of the signal entering the tube by electrically repelling some electrons, preventing their passage. Vacuum tubes were used as rectifiers to change an *alternating current* to a *direct current*, to amplify an electronic signal, or to act as an *oscillator*. Oscillators change a direct current into an alternating current of a particular frequency.

The vacuum tube revolutionized communications technology after British scientist John A. Fleming modified the one originally designed by American inventor Thomas A. Edison to intercept wireless radio signals. Improvements in vacuum tube manufacture soon led to the tubes' widespread use in many electronic devices. Though considered one of the most important inventions of the 20th century, they were fragile, expensive to produce, inefficient, and did not last long.

When Shockley started working at Bell, his job was to design an improved vacuum tube for amplifying electric signals. Radios depended on vacuum tubes to *rectify* and amplify antenna signals from radio waves. Shockley knew that the earliest radios utilized one *semiconductor*, galena, as a rectifier before vacuum tubes were developed. (Semiconductors are discussed later in this chapter.) He thought something solid might perform better and have wider applications than a vacuum tube, so he applied his expertise to begin developing a rectifying semiconductor. Unfortunately, the pure materials he required were not yet available, and the Second World War delayed his research.

During World War II, Shockley developed radar equipment for the military. He also served as research director of the U.S. Navy's Anti-Submarine Warfare Operations Research Group at Columbia University and as an expert consultant to the secretary of war. In 1945, he returned to industrial research as the director of Bell's solid-state physics research program, and he began collaborating with theoretical physicist John Bardeen and experimental physicist Walter H. Brattain. Shockley's goal was to replace the vacuum tube with a solid-state amplifier. The team spent one year unsuccessfully attempting to build Shockley's apparatus. When Bardeen suggested that electrons might get trapped on the surface rather than penetrate into the crystal, they went back to the drawing board to learn more about semiconductors.

## Semiconductors

Shockley still believed that a semiconductor could be used as an efficient electrical switch and to control the flow of an electrical current. Semiconductors are substances whose electrical conductivity is intermediate between good conductors, such as copper, and

### The Team

While Shockley was the originator of the concept of the transistor, a trio of scientists at Bell Laboratories brought the goal to fruition. Shockley shared the 1956 Nobel Prize in physics with John Bardeen and Walter Brattain for "their researches on semiconductors and their discovery of the transistor effect."

John Bardeen was born on May 23, 1908, in Madison, Wisconsin. He obtained a degree in electrical engineering from the University of Wisconsin in 1928. He continued his studies as a graduate research assistant working on mathematical problems in applied geophysics and on radiation from antennas. After two years, he moved to Pittsburgh, Pennsylvania, to work at the Gulf Research Laboratories, where he investigated magnetics and gravitational surveys for three years. In 1933, he

insulators, such as plastic, that block currents. An electrical current is simply a flow of electrons through a conductive material. Semiconductors are ideal for electronic uses because they allow for control over the amount and direction of flow. Germanium was once popular, but silicon is the most widely used semiconductor today. A single atom of silicon contains four electrons in the outermost, or *valence*, shell. These electrons can each participate in a covalent chemical bond with valence electrons from neighboring silicon atoms—one above, one below, and one on each side. When they do so, they form a crystal lattice. The overlapping energy shells combine to form energy bands (analogous to the energy shells of a single atom), with the highest band containing electrons being called the valence band. The band one level higher is called the conduction band. During conduction of an electric current through the semiconductor, an electron moves to an unoccupied energy

---

resumed his graduate studies on the theory of the work function of metals at Princeton University and earned a doctorate degree in mathematical physics in 1936. He next served as a fellow at Harvard University, then as assistant professor of physics at the University of Minnesota, and as a civilian physicist at the Naval Ordnance Laboratory in Washington, D.C., before he landed at Bell Laboratories in 1945. Bardeen was awarded a second Nobel Prize in physics in 1972, an honor he shared with Leon Neil Cooper and John Robert Schrieffer for their jointly developed theory of superconductivity, usually called the BCS-theory. Bardeen died on January 30, 1991.

Walter H. Brattain was born on February 10, 1902, in Amoy, China, but grew up on the family ranch in the state of Washington. He earned a bachelor of science degree in 1924 from Whitman College, a master of arts degree in 1926 from the University of Oregon, and a Ph.D. in physics from the University of Minnesota in 1929. After obtaining his doctorate, he accepted a position at Bell Laboratories, where his major research focus was the surface properties of solids. He died on October 13, 1987.

level, leaving behind a hole that can be filled by another electron moving into that empty position.

*Doping* is a process whereby impurities are added to the otherwise pure semiconductor in order to modify its conduction properties. For example, boron may be added to silicon. Boron has one less valence electron than silicon, thus the doped semiconductor contains an overall shortage of electrons. This type of semiconductor is called a P-semiconductor, because the lack of electrons effectively acts like an extra positive charge, though it should be noted that the semiconductor retains a net charge of zero. In P-type semiconductors, holes carry the current through the solid. In the process of N-doping, the added impurity has one more electron in its valence shell compared to silicon, making it easier for electrons to make the jump up to the conduction band. The element phosphorus, which has five valence electrons, is an example of an N-type dopant. In N-type semiconductors, negatively charged electrons carry the current. The amount of dopant is very tiny—roughly one atom per 10,000,000 atoms of the semiconductor.

## The First Transistor

Bardeen and Brattain announced their success in building the first transistor (named by combining the terms *transfer* and *resistor*) at a press conference during the summer of 1948. In order to understand how it functioned, consider the following. When a P-type and an N-type semiconductor are placed next to one another to create a P-N junction, there is an excess of electrons on the N side of the junction and a deficiency on the P side. This formation is called a *diode*, and the current can flow in only one direction. When the diode is connected to a battery such that the positive pole is connected to the P side and the negative pole is connected to the N side, the electrons and the holes in the semiconductors are drawn toward the P-N junction. The nearness allows the electrons to jump into the holes, and current flows through the diode. If the battery is connected in the reverse order, then no current will flow. Diodes are used as detectors in television and radio receivers and to convert alternating currents to direct currents.

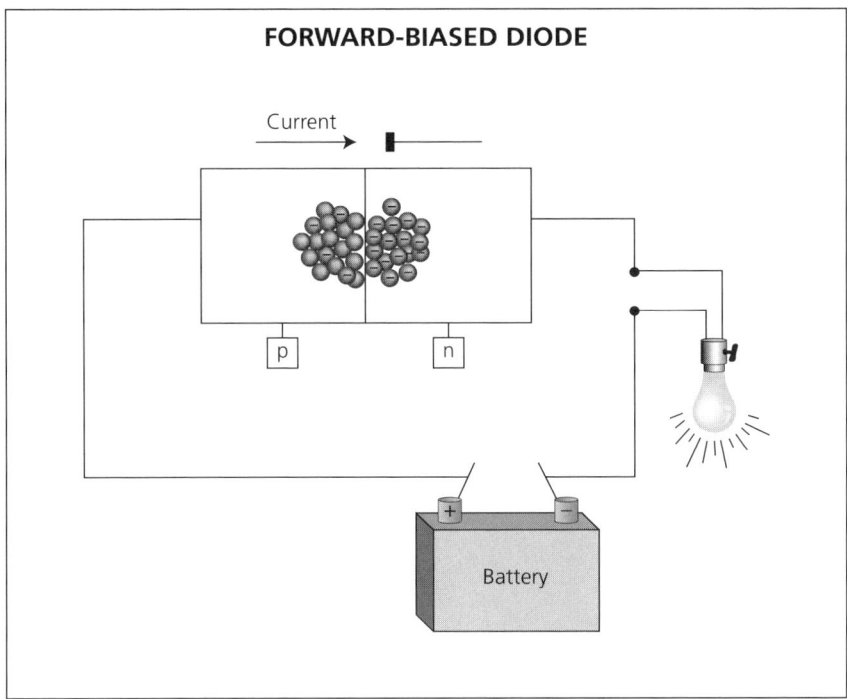

In a forward-biased diode, the electrons and holes gather near the P-N junction, where their proximity to one another allows the electrons to jump into the holes.

Bardeen and Brattain had built a point contact transistor that consisted of a block of N-type germanium, two gold contacts on one face of the crystal, and a tungsten base on the opposite side. This transistor was actually a triode, since there were three electrical terminals compared to two in a diode. One gold point contact was connected to a battery creating a forward-biased circuit; the other was reverse-biased. The gold contact where the current entered the semiconductor (on the forward-biased side) was called the emitter, and the other gold contact (on the reverse-biased side) was called the collector. The contact at the metal base acted as the base-electrode. Having two gold contacts allowed some control over the circuit. When voltage was applied, holes in the germanium near the emitter gold contact flowed to the collector, amplifying the signal at the collector in the process.

Within a few months, Shockley suggested improvements that led to the junction transistor that was first built in 1951. He proposed

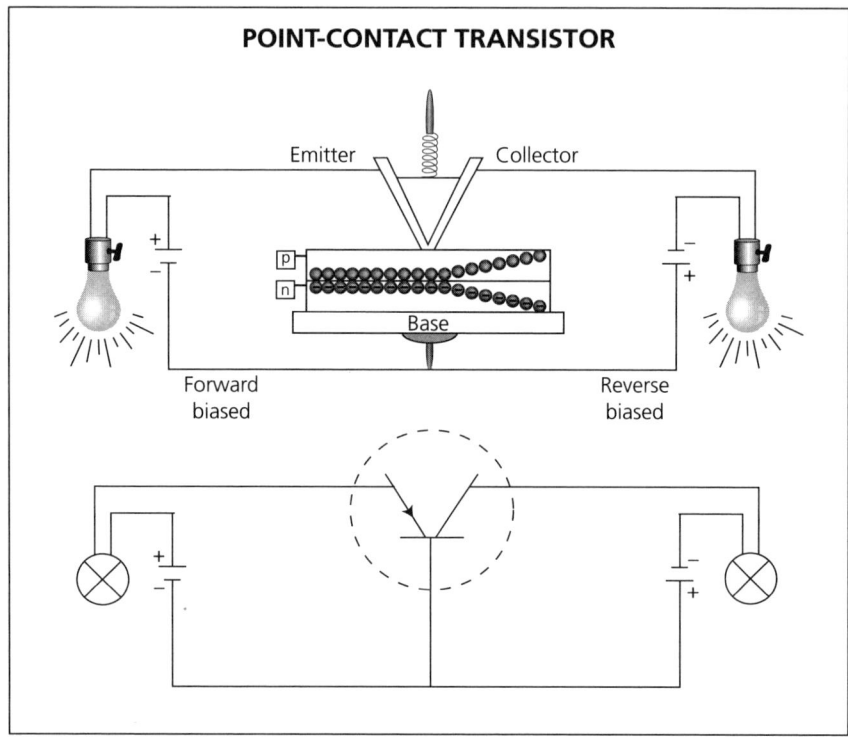

No current flows in a reverse-biased circuit alone, but when paired with a forward-biased circuit in a triode, activation occurs.

sandwiching a thin P-region between two N-regions to create an NPN junction and giving all the regions separate contacts. When a positive voltage was applied to the collector, the current flowed into the transistor through the collector, through the base, and out the emitter. Applying a small current to the base restricted the flow through the transistor, while amplification could be achieved by applying a large current to the base, supplying extra charge carriers. By the early 1950s, the junction transistor already was being used in hearing aids, radios, and microphones. The junction transistor eventually evolved into the more modern field-effect transistors (FETs) that also have three electric terminals but operate in a slightly different manner. Shockley, Bardeen, and Brattain shared the Nobel Prize in physics in 1956 for their research on semiconductors and their discovery of the transistor effect.

## Controversy

In 1954, Shockley resigned from Bell Laboratories and served as deputy director and research director for the Weapon System Evaluation Group of the Defense Department for one year. After moving his family to Palo Alto, California, he founded the Shockley Semiconductor Laboratory, later named the Shockley Transistor Corporation. The company was sold a few times and closed in 1969. He began consulting for Bell Labs again in 1965. Shockley's first marriage had ended in divorce in 1955, and he married Emily I. Lanning.

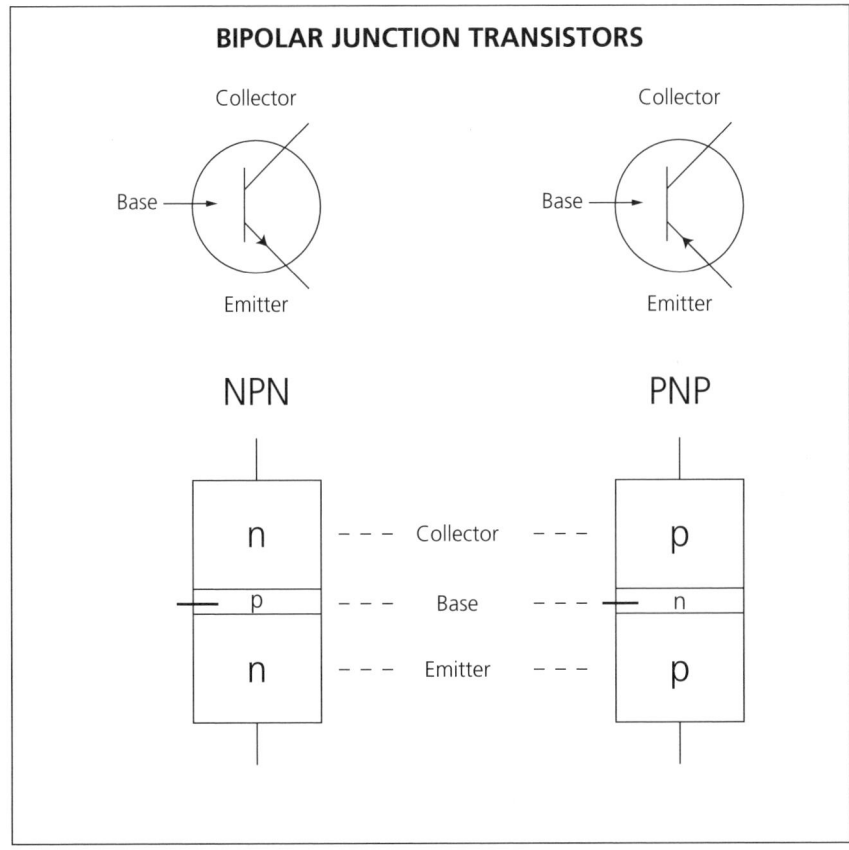

A bipolar junction transistor contains an opposed pair of P-N diodes in a single crystal.

Stanford University appointed Shockley the first Alexander M. Poniatoff Professor of Engineering and Applied Sciences in 1962. He taught electrical engineering at Stanford until he became a professor emeritus of electrical engineering in 1972, but his time there was marked by his controversial pronouncements concerning the relationship between race and intelligence. Though he never received formal training in a related field, he formulated the outrageous opinion that African Americans were not as naturally intelligent as Caucasians. He went further to suggest that more "white" genes would give an African American a greater mental capacity. Atrociously, he recommended that people with IQs lower than 100 be paid to undergo surgical *sterilization* in order to improve the human race. Though psychologists and educators rejected his conclusions, the offensive implications incited much controversy. Students protested in his classes, and his scientific reputation was called into question.

## Initiation of the Computer Revolution

William Shockley died from prostrate cancer on August 12, 1989, in Palo Alto, California. Though actions during his later years marred his reputation, Shockley's expertise in electrical engineering and his ability to solve problems stimulated the computer revolution. He obtained more than 90 patents for his valuable inventions, and many academic organizations honored his achievements. He received the Morris Leibmann Memorial Prize from the Institute of Radio Engineers in 1952, the Oliver E. Buckley Solid-State Physics Prize from the American Physical Society in 1953, the National Academy of Sciences Comstock Prize in 1954, the American Society of Mechanical Engineers Holley Medal in 1962, the Institute of Electrical and Electronic Engineers Gold Medal in 1972, and their Medal of Honor in 1980. He received the U.S. Medal of Merit in 1946 for his work with the war department, was appointed to the President's Scientific Advisory Committee in 1962, and was named to the National Inventors Hall of Fame in 1974. Shockley also was awarded honorary doctorate degrees from the University of Pennsylvania, Rutgers University, and Gustavus Adolphus College in Minnesota.

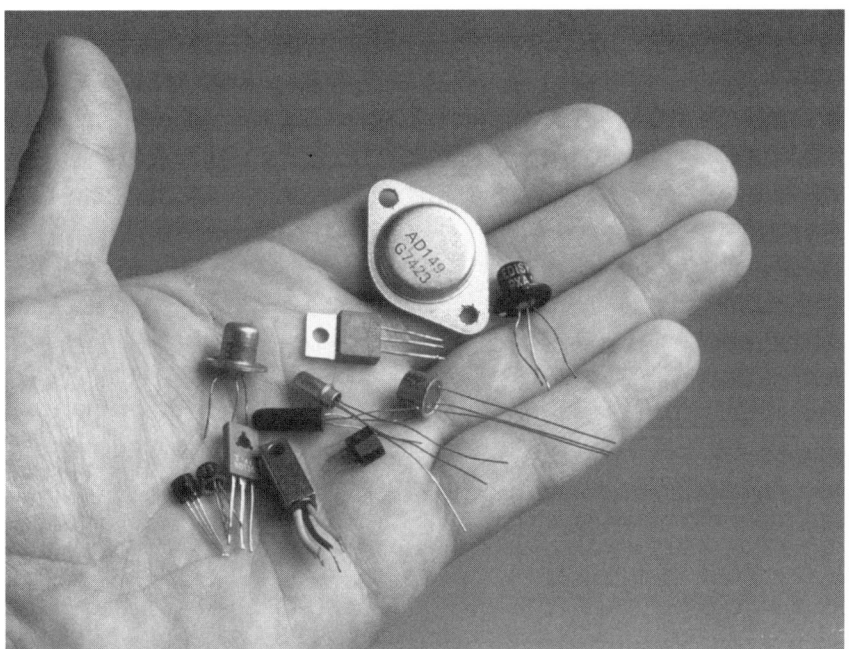

Transistors, such as these examples from the 1960s to 1990s, have allowed the miniaturization of electronic components. *(Tony Craddock/Photo Researchers, Inc.)*

Shockley's transistor was a revolutionary invention; however, it was bulky and difficult to produce en masse. Contemporary field-effect transistors (FETs) are used more generally. The type most commonly found in personal computers, metal oxide semiconductor field effect transistors (MOSFETs), contain different layers of doped silicon. Transistors range in size from $3.9 \times 10^{-5}$ inch (0.001 mm) to slightly less than one inch (2.54 cm) in width. Millions can be placed on tiny silicon chips called integrated circuits, microprocessors, or computer chips. Electronic circuits running through these computer chips carry out the work of computers, such as performing calculations and forming images on the monitor. Shockley passed away before the Internet became popularized, but he would no doubt have been pleased to see such a remarkable application of the technology he helped create. His invention of the transistor was responsible for the miniaturization of circuits and the affordability and reliability of the electronic devices we enjoy today.

# CHRONOLOGY

| | |
|---|---|
| 1910 | William Shockley is born on February 13 in London, England |
| 1932 | Receives a bachelor of science degree in physics from the California Institute of Technology |
| 1936 | Obtains a doctorate degree in physics from the Massachusetts Institute of Technology and starts working at Bell Telephone Laboratories |
| 1942–45 | Participates in war effort by researching radar and anti-submarine warfare and consulting to the secretary of war |
| 1945 | Returns to Bell Laboratories and researches the use of semiconductors to replace vacuum tubes |
| 1947 | Bardeen and Brattain build the first successful point contact transistor |
| 1951 | Shockley's junction transistor is built |
| 1955 | Leaves Bell Laboratories and starts own company, Shockley Semiconductor Laboratory, later named Shockley Transistor Corporation |
| 1956 | Shockley shares the Nobel Prize in physics with Bardeen and Brattain for their research on semiconductors and for developing the transistor |
| 1962 | Becomes the first Alexander M. Poniatoff Professor of Engineering and Applied Sciences at Stanford University |
| 1972 | Retires from Stanford University |
| 1989 | On August 12, Shockley dies from prostate cancer at age 79, in Palo Alto, California |

# FURTHER READING

*Biographical Memoirs of Fellows of the Royal Society.* Vol. 68. London: The Royal Society, 1996. Authoritative, full memoir written by a distinguished colleague; includes a complete bibliography.

*Encyclopedia of World Biography, Second Edition.* Vol. 14. Detroit: Gale Research, 1998. Brief biographies of notable figures and summaries of their accomplishments. Written for high school students.

Garraty, John A., and Mark C. Carnes, eds. *American National Biography.* Vol. 19. New York: Oxford University Press, 1999. Brief accounts of the lives and work of famous Americans in encyclopedia format.

Nobelprize.org. "The Nobel Prize in Physics 1956." Available online. URL: http://www.nobelprize.org/physics/laureates/1956. Last modified on June 16, 2000. Contains links for Shockley's biography, his Nobel lecture, and other related resources.

Saari, Peggy, and Stephen Allison, eds. *The Lives and Works of 150 Scientists.* Vol. 3. Detroit: U*X*L, 1996. Alphabetically arranged introductions to the contributions of scientists from a variety of fields. Appropriate for middle school students.

# Patrick C. Steptoe

(1913–1988)

Obstetrician Patrick Steptoe pioneered assisted reproductive technology by performing the first human in vitro fertilization. *(National Portrait Gallery, London)*

## Pioneer of In Vitro Fertilization

The Centers for Disease Control and Prevention estimated that for the year 2001, more than 40,000 babies were born in the United States as a result of assisted reproductive technology (ART). The American Society for Reproductive Medicine estimates that more than 6 million people in the United States, almost 10 percent of the reproductive age population, have fertility problems. The number of couples seeking treatment for *infertility*, medically defined as the inability to conceive after one year of unprotected intercourse or the inability to carry a pregnancy to term, has steadily increased since ART was introduced in the United States in 1981. Previously, women with blocked *oviducts*, the tubes connecting the ovaries to the *uterus*, were told they could never have a baby biologically their own, but with the advent of ART, now they may have a success rate higher than that of a woman who tries to conceive naturally. Dr. Patrick Steptoe spent a decade pioneering *in vitro fertilization* (IVF), a technique that forms the basis of many ART procedures, in collaboration with Robert G. Edwards, producing the world's first "test-tube baby" in 1978.

# A Royal Navy Volunteer

Patrick Christopher Steptoe was born on June 9, 1913, in rural Witney, Oxfordshire, England. His father, Harry Arthur Steptoe, was registrar of births, deaths, and marriages in Witney and an organist for a local church. His mother, Grace Maud Mimms Steptoe, was a social worker involved in family planning. She organized the local Mothers' Union and Infant Welfare Clinics, in addition to raising Patrick and his seven siblings. Later in life, Steptoe credited his mother for her encouragement and for imparting the lesson of perseverance over obstacles. Patrick studied music during his youth and even played the piano for silent films at the local cinema. He attributed his manual strength and dexterity, which would be important for his surgical career, to the countless hours he spent practicing the piano. Though he was an accomplished pianist, he chose to study medicine.

After graduating from King's College in London, Steptoe attended St. George's Hospital Medical School at the University of London. He obtained his diploma and license to practice medicine from the Royal College of Physicians in 1939 and became a member of the Royal College of Surgeons. Steptoe began his medical career as a volunteer surgeon in the Royal Navy during World War II. The Italian forces captured him in 1941 when his ship sank near Crete, and he was placed in solitary confinement for helping other prisoners escape. In 1943, he was released in a prisoner exchange.

Steptoe married Sheena Kennedy, the daughter of a physician, upon demobilization in 1946. They had two children together, Sally and Andrew, and remained married until Steptoe's death.

## Development of Laparoscopic Surgery

After returning to London, Steptoe fulfilled the necessary requirements to specialize in obstetrics and gynecology. *Obstetricians* are physicians whose expertise is pregnancy and birth, whereas *gynecologists* specialize in more generalized care of the female reproduction system. From 1947 to 1949, Steptoe was the chief assistant in obstetrics and gynecology at St. George's Hospital, and then he worked for two years as the senior registrar at the Whittington Hospital. He became a member of the Royal College of Obstetricians and Gynecologists in 1948 and a fellow in 1961. He became a fellow of the Royal College of Surgeons in 1950.

In 1951, Steptoe accepted a consultant position with the National Health Service at the Oldham and District General Hospital in Lancashire. The area desperately needed the services of a qualified obstetrician/gynecologist, and Steptoe spent his first few years removing tumors and dealing with other dangerous medical conditions that had been left untreated for too long due to the backlog. He established a family planning clinic and then began investigating methods for sterilization, a procedure that renders a person incapable of reproducing.

After becoming well established, Steptoe also became interested in infertility, a condition that is caused by numerous different factors and decreases a couple's chance for conception. One major cause is natural blockage of the oviducts, which can result from a previous sexually transmitted disease or infection, such as chlamydia, or endometriosis, a painful condition in which tissue that normally is found inside the uterus implants outside the uterus. While in Oldham, Steptoe became frustrated by having to perform numerous diagnostic laparotomies, a procedure he considered excessive, in which the abdominal cavity is surgically opened up so the physician can see and feel everything inside. Recovery from a laparotomy was difficult, and often nothing abnormal was found. He pioneered a procedure called *laparoscopy*, in which the surgeon performs minimally invasive surgery by inserting a sterile, long, skinny telescope with a built-in light into the abdomen through a tiny incision. Usually the cavity is distended with air to aid in viewing the organs and to provide space for manipulating surgical instruments. In this manner, the physician can observe the condition of the patient's internal organs, including the ovaries, oviducts, and uterus, and diagnose possible causes for infertility, such as endometriosis or cysts.

Steptoe became an expert in the use of a laparoscope for surgical procedures; he could skillfully explore the oviducts and obtain specimens from inside the abdomen. He also performed laparoscopic surgical sterilizations by destroying a piece of each oviduct with an electric current, then later by applying tubal clips. In cases where a man's sperm count was too low to impregnate his wife, Steptoe directly introduced spermatozoa into her oviducts, but this never resulted in a successful pregnancy. His peers in the United Kingdom thought laparoscopy was too problematic and were slow to recognize its advantages, mainly that recovery time was greatly reduced compared with an exploratory surgery requiring much larger incisions. Steptoe spent five years perfecting the technique before he published his first paper on laparoscopic surgery, in 1965, "Gynecological Endoscopy—Laparoscopy and Culdoscopy," in the *Journal of Obstetrics and Gynaecology of the British Commonwealth*. The unenthusiastic response of his British colleagues disappointed Steptoe, who proceeded to write an entire textbook, *Laparoscopy in Gynaecology* (1967), devoted to this technique and enormously influential in introducing laparoscopy to the United States.

# A Complementary Partnership

In 1967, Steptoe received a phone call from Robert G. Edwards, a physiologist from Cambridge University who specialized in the female reproductive system and who had seen an article authored by Steptoe, "Laparoscopy and Ovulation," in *The Lancet* (1968). Edwards had been studying fertility problems and was trying to fertilize human eggs outside the body, using eggs he obtained from ovaries that had been surgically removed for medical reasons. He contacted Steptoe in hopes of acquiring maturing oocytes (eggs) and sperm from a woman's oviducts. These sperm would have been exposed to the secretions found in the female reproductive tract and might have undergone some unknown transformation required for fertilization.

The two met six months later at a meeting of the Endocrinological and Gynecological section of the Royal Society of Medicine in London. They began collaborating at Oldham General Hospital in 1968, and Steptoe provided a small room in the pathology department for Edwards to set up a research laboratory. Their ultimate goal was to help women with blocked oviducts become pregnant by fertilizing her egg in a petri dish, then putting it back into her body to implant in the uterus and develop into a healthy baby. Plenty of women who had trouble with blocked oviducts volunteered for their research in hopes of having a child of their own. Edwards resided 200 miles (322 km) away, in Cambridge, but whenever Steptoe called to say that ovarian tissue would be available, he drove to Oldham to use the eggs for his research. Sometimes when performing hysterectomies, Steptoe collected sperm from the reproductive tract for Edwards to study.

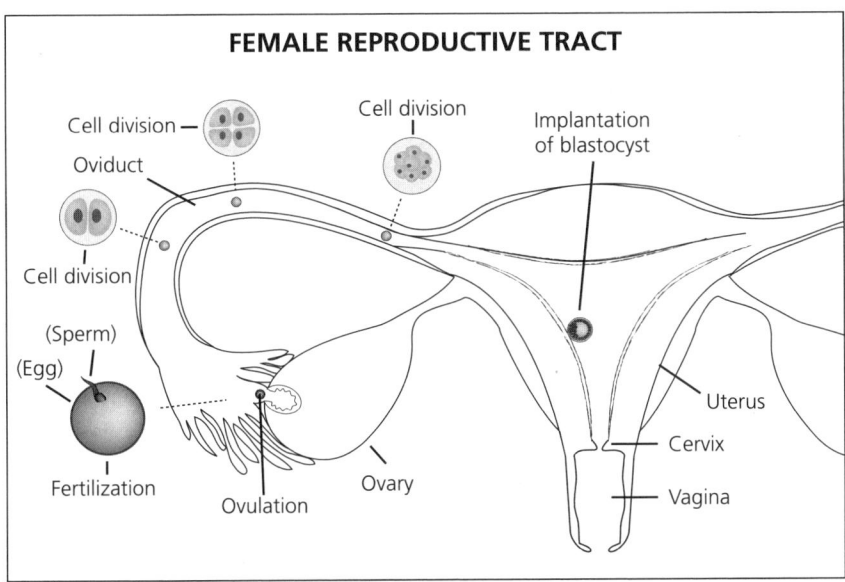

Each month, one ovary releases a mature egg that moves down the oviduct, where it may be fertilized by a single sperm cell, travel to the uterus, and implant in the lining.

Using laparoscopy, Steptoe was able to locate and aspirate mature eggs from a woman's ovaries at the time in her menstrual cycle that she naturally ovulated, when the *ovary* normally released a mature egg into the oviduct. Injections of follicle-stimulating hormone (FSH) induced the women's ovaries to *superovulate*, producing several eggs for Steptoe to harvest. Edwards would then attempt to fertilize the eggs with human sperm in a petri dish. He learned that sperm did not require exposure to the female reproductive tract in order to be capable of fertilizing an egg in vitro, but the sperm did require washing, and the composition of the culture media was critical. Though the sperm itself performed the complicated task of penetrating the egg and depositing its genetic material inside, Edwards had to determine and simulate the optimal physiological conditions for the successful union. In other words, he had to mimic the conditions inside the oviducts with respect to temperature, salinity, pH, sugars, amino acids, and other nutrients in order to preserve the integrity of both of the *gametes*, the eggs and sperm.

## Initial Promising Results

In 1968, the duo achieved their first goal when Edwards fertilized a human egg in vitro. In 1969, they reported their success in "Early Stages of Human Fertilization In Vitro of Human Oocytes Matured In Vitro," in the journal *Nature*. The eggs were from ovaries that Steptoe had removed from women and then placed in a sterile dish to which the hormone human chorionic *gonadotropin* was added to induce ripening, or maturation, of the eggs. Edwards added sperm about 36 hours later and found evidence of sperm entering the eggs 10 to 12 hours afterward. They still had a long way to go before achieving the ultimate goal of a healthy baby. The next step was obtaining cleavage of a fertilized egg in the laboratory.

They started using eggs ripened in vivo that Steptoe removed by aspiration using laparoscopy. After a sperm penetrated an egg, they transferred the *zygote* to another dish containing a slightly different solution, optimized for the many rounds of cell division the zygote must undergo as it develops into an embryo. After 18 months, they obtained embryos that had reached the *blastocyst* stage, the stage occurring approximately four and one-half days after fertilization, when the cluster of cells normally implants into the lining of the uterus.

Steptoe and Edwards applied for a grant from the Medical Research Council (MRC) to set up a clinic and laboratory near Cambridge, but the MRC denied their application on ethical grounds. The Oldham Area Health Authority generously offered Steptoe and Edwards space at Kershaw's Cottage Hospital in nearby Royton, where they set up an IVF clinic including an operating facility and a small research laboratory.

## Perseverance through Failures

By the end of 1971, they felt confident that only one sperm was penetrating each egg and that early development was proceeding normally. They were ready to attempt replanting an embryo into the mother. Steptoe attempted replanting an embryo at the eight-cell stage using a thin, sterile plastic tube inserted through the

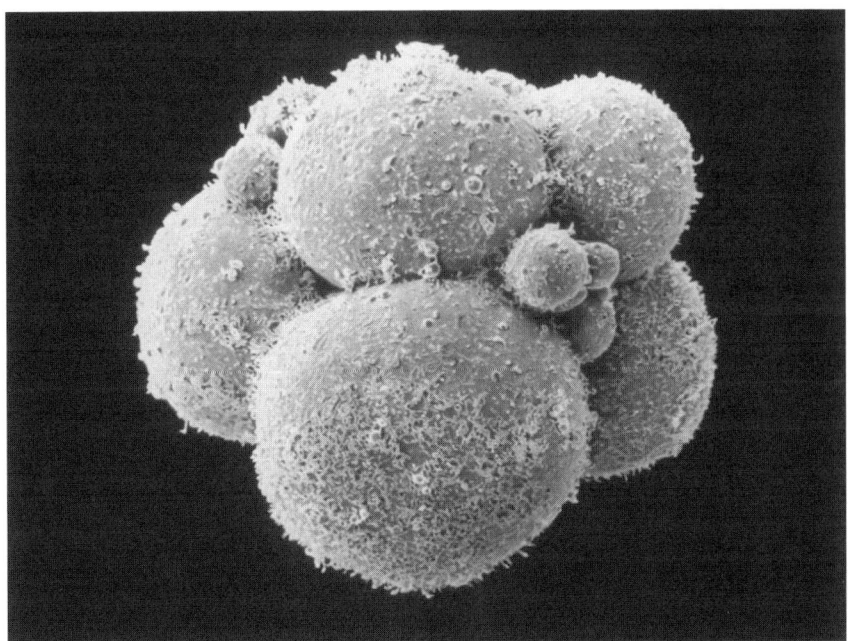

At the eight-cell stage, a human embryo has not yet implanted in the uterus. *(Dr. Yorgos Nikas/Photo Researchers, Inc.)*

cervix into the uterus for the first time in early 1972, but the process was not successful. Others thought keeping the fertilized eggs cultured in the laboratory for several days before *implantation* was the problem, but Steptoe and Edwards did not agree, because the zygotes developed into morphologically normal blastocysts. They thought that the fertility drugs that the women received to induce the ripening of multiple eggs were shortening the length of their menstrual cycles, so that by the time the embryo was placed back into the mother, the uterus was already preparing to shed its lining, preventing implantation from ever occurring. They tried treating the women with gonadotropins, then *estrogen* and *progesterone*, to overcome this problem. A decade later their research would show that some of the hormones they administered to the women to help establish pregnancy actually prevented embryonic growth. After no successes they abandoned the steroid hormone treatments in 1974.

The summer of 1975 brought the first positive pregnancy test. The additional hormone treatments might have helped, but they could not be sure. Disappointingly, the pregnancy was *ectopic*, meaning the embryo implanted in the oviduct rather than in the uterus, and Steptoe had to immediately remove the conceptus. Other women also became pregnant, but none of the pregnancies lasted past the first trimester.

By the summer of 1977, Steptoe and Edwards agreed to attempt the process without the assistance of fertility drugs. This meant they would have only a single egg to fertilize in the laboratory, as well as need to monitor the woman's natural menstrual cycle so they knew when that precious egg would be mature. Edwards planned to measure levels of luteinizing hormone in the urine as an indicator of when the egg would be ready for harvesting.

As the two struggled to overcome the mechanistic obstacles in their research, they also endured attacks by the clergy, other scientists, and the public who believed what they were doing was ethically wrong. Opponents expressed concern over the scientists "playing God," risking the creation of abnormal babies, the consequences of possible selective breeding, and the destruction of numerous embryos in the course of their research. The British parliament launched an investigation and cut off research funding for Steptoe and Edwards, suggesting they needed to perform more preliminary experiments on other primates. Meanwhile, Steptoe performed legal medical abortions in order to obtain funding for their research. The two did their best to avoid the limelight and the public, but their secrecy aroused even more suspicion and criticism.

## Success!

In 1976, Lesley Brown, a 30-year-old woman with blocked oviducts who had been trying to conceive for nine years, sought Steptoe's assistance in becoming pregnant. The following year Steptoe performed surgery on Brown to remove her diseased oviducts and several adhesions from her pelvic cavity. On November 10, 1977, Steptoe used an electric aspirating pump to gently remove a single ripened egg from her left ovary. Edwards added the egg to prepared sperm from her husband. Two and one-half days later, Steptoe replanted the eight-cell embryo into Brown's uterus. Everyone was elated when, after a few weeks, Brown still had not begun to menstruate. Repeated tests confirmed a positive pregnancy. An in vitro fertilized egg had implanted! This was a medical miracle. At the end of the first trimester, genetic testing revealed Brown was carrying a chromosomally normal female fetus. Brown developed toxemia, which threatened her health and the health of the baby, so Steptoe performed a Cesarean section to deliver the full-term baby. On July 25, 1978, in Oldham, Louise Joy Brown was born, weighing in at five pounds, 12 ounces (2.6 kg). She was normal and healthy and cried immediately.

Steptoe and Edwards did not immediately publish their results in the scientific literature, but they held a press conference two days after delivering Baby Louise. They did not share details of their research, but assured the press that in vitro fertilization would soon be a common practice for treating infertility. In October 1978, Steptoe was supposed to receive an award from the Barren Foundation, a Chicago Fertility Research Organization, but the foundation canceled before the date because the scientists still had not published their results in a scientific journal. Steptoe responded by saying that scientists normally did not publish results of their work until up to a year after they completed their research. Reports in the popular press accused Steptoe of accepting a large amount of money from a tabloid for his story. Steptoe denied the allegation and claimed that he had not made any money from the highly publicized birth. The Browns, however, accepted a contract with a newspaper for their story, as was their right.

On January 26, 1979, Steptoe and Edwards presented a full account of their research and the IVF procedure at the Royal College of Obstetricians and Gynecologists meeting in London, where they received the first-ever standing ovation at the college. A week later at the American Fertility Society conference in San Francisco, California, Steptoe received another standing ovation and a commendation plaque.

## Modern ART

Though 85 percent to 90 percent of infertile couples can be treated successfully by the administration of drugs or by surgical repair of reproductive organs, others require more complicated treatment to conceive and deliver a live baby. Assisted reproductive technology (ART) generally refers to procedures that involve the handling of both eggs and sperm, so procedures such as the administration of medicine by itself or simple artificial insemination, where sperm are injected into a woman's cervix, are not included. Three common ART procedures include in vitro fertilization (IVF), gamete intrafallopian transfer (GIFT), and zygote intrafallopian transfer (ZIFT).

The procedure pioneered by Steptoe and Edwards, IVF, forms the basis of all three techniques and accounts for 98 percent of ART procedures. IVF benefits women who have blocked or absent oviducts and men who have low sperm counts. Usually the woman is given ovulation-inducing drugs to stimulate the ripening or maturation of multiple eggs within her ovaries. After two intense weeks of carefully orchestrated

Three other women became pregnant shortly after Brown. One woman miscarried within a few weeks, and another couple lost their baby after the mother delivered prematurely at just over 20 weeks gestation, but the third pregnancy resulted in a healthy baby boy named Alastair.

## Hope for Millions

Steptoe retired from the British National Health Service in 1978 and opened a private IVF clinic near Cambridge that he directed until his death. By 1986, Steptoe had assisted in almost 1,000 conceptions at

---

treatments with fertility drugs, the physician retrieves the eggs by aspiration through a needle guided by ultrasound. The hopeful father provides a fresh sperm specimen that is washed and added to a dish containing the harvested eggs in a specially designed culture medium, and the gametes are incubated together for 14 to 18 hours. By this time, the sperm have penetrated the eggs, and the zygotes are placed in a new culture medium optimized for cell division. After one and one-half to five days, depending on the clinic, the physician uses a microscope to select the healthiest embryos and places them inside the uterus, using a catheter inserted through the vagina and cervix. Administration of the steroid hormone progesterone helps prepare the uterine lining for implantation.

GIFT begins the same way as IVF; the woman is given drugs to induce ovulation, and the eggs are retrieved and combined with a prepared sperm sample. The difference is that in GIFT, immediately following egg retrieval, the eggs and sperm are combined and placed together in the oviduct, the site where fertilization naturally occurs, using a laparoscope. Of course, the woman must have at least one open oviduct for this to work. Using GIFT, a physician never knows if fertilization occurred. In ZIFT, the egg is fertilized in the laboratory, and then returned to the oviduct before undergoing cell division. The physician cannot know whether the zygote developed into a normal blastocyst.

the Bourn Hall Clinic. Eventually Steptoe's work was applauded, IVF became a routine procedure worldwide, and both he and Edwards were named commanders of the Order of the British Empire in 1988. The Royal Society elected Steptoe a fellow in 1987, and he received gold medals from the Royal College of Obstetricians and Gynecologists in 1985 and the British Medicine Association in 1988. Steptoe was also honored by the American Academy of Achievement, the New York Fertility Society, and the American Fertility Society, among others. He had served as president of the International Federation of Fertility Societies (1977) and as the first chairman of the British Fertility Society (1974–86).

Patrick Steptoe passed away from prostate cancer on March 21, 1988, in Canterbury, England, and was buried in a Bourn churchyard. His work is remembered and appreciated by millions. Today, physicians commonly perform laparoscopy, the procedure pioneered by Steptoe, to diagnose causes of abdominal pain or infertility, and the patient returns home within a few hours. Hundreds of thousands of children have been born worldwide through IVF. Though some still consider conception by IVF unnatural and immoral, those who have directly benefited from the process developed by Steptoe and Edwards consider the technology nothing less than a miracle.

In the early 1980s, a 17-year-old boy underwent treatment for testicular cancer, leaving him infertile. Before initiating treatment, he had samples of his sperm frozen in liquid nitrogen, and 21 years later, a scientist thawed his sperm and injected single sperm cells into harvested eggs. Through IVF, he was able to have a son, thanks to Patrick Steptoe, the physician who persevered through technological obstacles and social criticism to give infertile couples hope.

## CHRONOLOGY

| | |
|---|---|
| 1913 | Patrick Steptoe is born on June 9 in Witney, Oxfordshire, England |
| 1935–39 | Attends St. George Hospital Medical School at the University of London |
| 1939 | Obtains a license to practice medicine and joins the Royal College of Surgeons |

| | |
|---|---|
| 1939–46 | Serves in the Royal Navy |
| 1947–49 | Is chief assistant in obstetrics and gynecology at St. George's Hospital |
| 1948 | Becomes a member of the Royal College of Obstetricians and Gynecologists |
| 1949–51 | Starts working at the Oldham General and District Hospital in Lancashire |
| 1961 | Becomes a fellow of the Royal College of Obstetricians and Gynecologists |
| 1965 | Publishes first paper on laparoscopic surgery |
| 1968 | Begins collaborating with physiologist Robert Edwards. First egg is fertilized in vitro |
| 1972 | Attempts first implantation of eggs fertilized in vitro |
| 1978 | First "test-tube baby" is born. Steptoe retires from the British National Health Service to open a private clinic near Cambridge |
| 1988 | Dies of prostate cancer on March 21 in Canterbury, England |

## FURTHER READING

*Biographical Memoirs of Fellows of the Royal Society of London.* Vol. 42. London: Royal Society, 1996. Authoritative, full memoir written by Steptoe's close collaborator and friend, Robert G. Edwards.

Edwards, R. G., and Patrick Steptoe. *A Matter of Life: The Story of a Medical Breakthrough.* New York: William Morrow and Company, 1980. The inside story of the development of IVF as told by the two scientists responsible.

"Infertility." MedlinePlus. Available online. URL: http://www.nlm.nih.gov/medlineplus/infertility.html. Last updated on March 7, 2005. Published by the U.S. National Library of Medicine and the National Institutes of Health, this site contains current information on diagnosis, anatomy and physiology, treatment, and statistics related to infertility.

Moritz, Charles, ed., *Current Biography Yearbook 1979.* New York: H. W. Wilson Company, 1980. Brief biographies of worldwide newsmakers.

Saari, Peggy, and Stephen Allison, eds. *The Lives and Works of 150 Scientists.* Vol. 3. Detroit: U*X*L, 1996. Alphabetically arranged introductions to the contributions of scientists from a variety of fields. Appropriate for middle school students.

# 9

# Kary B. Mullis

(1944– )

Kary Mullis developed the concept of the polymerase chain reaction, a biotechnological tool that stimulated tremendous advancements in cellular and molecular biological research and genetic engineering.
(© *The Nobel Foundation*)

## Invention of the Polymerase Chain Reaction

Mentioning the name Kary Mullis in a room full of distinguished scientists might bring groans or sighs of frustration. Mullis, a corecipient of the 1993 Nobel Prize in chemistry, is an interesting character to say the least; he is admittedly wild, pompous, and unconventional. The day he learned that he won the Nobel Prize, he dodged reporters and went surfing, and he escorted both his ex-wife and his girlfriend to the Nobel ceremony. Mullis offered a unique solution to the problem of isolating and amplifying specific fragments of *deoxyribonucleic acid* (DNA) from complex genomes—the *polymerase chain reaction* (PCR), a method for accurately reproducing tiny bits of sometimes hidden DNA millions of times within a few hours. His invention of this powerful technique advanced research in numerous fields, including medicine, genetics, biotechnology, and forensics. The wide range of PCR applications includes the detection of infectious organisms, DNA analysis for taxonomic classification, ecological studies on seed dispersal, genetic fingerprinting to identify criminal suspects, and limiting the illegal trade of endangered species. The possibilities for its use change daily.

## An Explosive Introduction to Chemistry

Kary B. Mullis was born on December 28, 1944, in Lenoir, North Carolina, to Bernice Alberta Barker Mullis and her husband, Cecil Banks Mullis. Kary was named after his great-grandfather, Cary, but with a spelling change so he would not share initials with his father, who was an institutional-furniture salesman. Kary spent his early childhood among dairy cows, chickens, hay, and peach trees at his grandparents' farm in the rural foothills of the Blue Ridge Mountains. He enjoyed summers cavorting with his brother in the woodshed and in the orchards, out in the Carolina sunshine.

Kary's first experience with science involved a chemistry set he received for Christmas and supplemented with chemicals purchased from the local drugstore. The enthusiasm shared by Kary and his friends delighted the chemistry teacher at Dreher High School in Columbia, South Carolina, where the Mullis family had lived since Kary was five years old, and she allowed them free reign in the laboratory after school hours. He figured out how to launch homemade rockets by heating concoctions of potassium nitrate and table sugar, once sending a live frog a mile into the sky. Kary, who was president of the Junior Engineering Technical Society, and a friend once put on a science demonstration for elementary students. In the opening moments during a pyrotechnic display, a crucible exploded. Nobody was hurt, but at least one young boy, who caught a piece of glass during the explosion, was turned on to chemistry. Later in life, Kary's characteristic wild behavior simultaneously awed aspiring scientists and disgusted his more traditional colleagues.

# A Winding Road to an Interesting Molecule

Kary entered the Georgia Institute of Technology and received a bachelor of science degree in chemistry in 1966. During the summers, he and a friend synthesized and sold organic chemicals to a supply company. They set up a lab in his friend's garage and specialized in making chemicals that other companies discontinued, sometimes because they were too dangerous to produce for the limited demand. They moved their lab into an old chicken coop after the friend's grandmother accidentally was teargassed upon entering the garage to do some laundry. Throughout his life, Kary blazed onward, enjoying the ride and leaving behind a trail of unfortunate events.

As an undergraduate, Mullis married a woman named Richards, who gave birth to a daughter, Louise. The University of California at Berkeley (UCB) accepted Mullis's application for graduate study in biochemistry, and the family moved west. His dissertation adviser, Joe Neilands, specialized in iron transport of microorganisms, but he encouraged his graduate students to explore their own interests. Mullis completed a dissertation titled "Structure and Organic Synthesis of Microbial Iron Transport Agents" in 1972. The members of his graduate committee hesitated to grant Mullis a doctorate degree but felt justified in doing so since Mullis already had published a paper in the prestigious journal *Nature* in 1968. Unrelated to his dissertation, the astrophysical paper, "The Cosmological Significance of Time Reversal," suggesting that half of the matter in the universe was going backward in time, reportedly was inspired by Mullis's "enhanced perception" of the cosmos while under the influence of hallucinogenic drugs. Mullis, by then divorced, remained at UCB for one year as a lecturer in biochemistry.

In 1973, Mullis moved to Kansas City, where his new second wife entered medical school at the University of Kansas (UK). She left him, and the following year he met and then married his third wife, Cynthia Gibson, a nurse with whom he had two sons, Christopher and Jeremy. In Kansas, Mullis attempted to write a novel but lacked inspiration, so he got a job researching the biochemistry of a chronic lung disorder in pediatric cardiology at the UK Medical Center. Mullis moved back to Berkeley, where he managed a restaurant and coffee shop for two years, then in 1977 he got a job at the University of California in San Francisco working on endorphins, a group of morphinelike chemicals in the brain that suppress pain and promote a feeling of well-being. Like his position at UK, the job was repetitive and below the level his credentials warranted, but it allowed him to reenter the research field. He had never been very interested in DNA, but after attending a seminar about the cloning of the somatostatin gene, the gene encoding a polypeptide hormone that regulates the secretion of other hormones such as growth hormone and insulin, Mullis became inspired to learn more about DNA and its synthesis.

DNA is a long chain of four *nucleotides* (A, C, G, and T), the sequence of which encodes for the synthesis of proteins within the cell. Each nucleotide specifically pairs with another nucleotide (A with T and C with G) in a manner that binds two strands of DNA to one another. This specific pairing means that if one knows the sequence of one strand of DNA, the sequence of the so-called *complementary* strand can be determined. In the cell, an enzyme called *DNA polymerase* performs the task of synthesizing new DNA molecules by reading one strand and incorporating complementary nucleotides to build the other strand.

## The Concentration Problem

In 1979, Mullis took a job as a DNA chemist at Cetus Corporation, in Emeryville, California, where he quickly learned about DNA synthesis and improved the efficiency of production of *oligonucleotides*, short stretches of single-stranded DNA. One of the groups at Cetus was trying to come up with a method for detecting point mutations, alterations to a single base pair on a molecule of DNA that can have devastating effects and are responsible for some inherited diseases. The *oligomer restriction* assay consisted of a series of simple steps to detect changes in a nucleotide sequence, but it was not very reliable or efficient. The first step was to heat the DNA sample in order to denature, or separate, the two complementary strands. The addition of a radioactively labeled oligonucleotide that was complementary to the denatured target DNA resulted in *hybridization* between the oligonucleotide and its complementary sequence on the *template* strand, a process resembling a zipping together of the two strands. If the DNA did not have a mutation, then subsequent treatment with an enzyme called a *restriction enzyme* would cut the DNA at a specific site. If the target DNA did have a point mutation, then the restriction enzyme would not cut it. Analysis of the DNA following this treatment revealed whether the sequence contained the mutation that caused a particular disease.

Mullis thought about improving the oligomer restriction assay by adding DNA polymerase to the tube in order to extend the oligonucleotide. The DNA polymerase would "read" the next unpaired nucleotide from the template strand and add the appropriate matching nucleotide. If he used a special type of nucleotide called a *dideoxynucleotide*, the polymerase would only add one single nucleotide to the oligonucleotide. By setting up four separate reactions, each containing a different radioactively labeled dideoxynucleotide, one could determine which nucleotide was present at the site of the putative mutation on the template strand. Mullis' technique for identifying point mutations worked on purified DNA samples, but the sensitivity of the technique was not sufficient if the region containing the specific sequence of interest was rare. While others pondered means to increase the final signal strength, Mullis wondered how he could increase the relative concentration of that one particular stretch of DNA.

This obstacle was on his mind on what has become a legendary Friday night in May of 1983, as Mullis was driving with his girlfriend to a cabin he owned in Mendocino. He thought that since oligonucleotides were cheap and easy to make, why not put two into the reaction, with one binding to each strand of the double-stranded DNA molecule? Due to the unique directionality of the two complementary DNA strands, each oligonucleotide would direct synthesis toward the other. If the oligonucleotides were different initial lengths, Mullis could separate them later, and one could act as a control for the other. Though this procedure sounds rather complex, it is based on sound principles of known processes and is technically simple to perform in the laboratory.

Mullis had not yet solved the concentration problem but was feeling proud of himself for thinking of a cheap and useful control mechanism for his experiments. While pondering potential complications, he considered the possibility of contaminating nucleotides in the mixture. If nucleotides other than the special dideoxynucleotides were present, then results would be difficult to analyze. To remove the contaminating building blocks, he could incubate the sample with DNA polymerase to use them all up, and then heat the reaction mixture to separate the DNA strands. Cooling the mixture would allow fresh, unextended oligonucleotides to hybridize to the target sequence, and the subsequent addition of the dideoxynucleotides and fresh DNA polymerase should overcome the problem. The thought then occurred to him that if the newly extended oligonucleotides were long enough, they also might hybridize to the unextended oligonucleotides added in the second round. One problem kept leading to another, and he began to wonder if his idea was hopeless. What was the likely outcome of this new contrived scenario? Mullis suddenly realized the outcome would be the same—the sequence of the DNA in the target and in the extended oligonucleotides would be identical, but the concentration of the DNA of interest would be doubled. By purposefully adding what he had previously considered annoying "contaminating" nucleotides, he could ensure this happened, and the process could be repeated over and over. The first round of DNA polymerase action would double the amount of target DNA, two rounds would quadruple it, three rounds would increase it by a factor of eight, and so on. After 10 cycles, one million times the original amount of DNA would be present. Mullis not only solved the concentration problem, but in a breakthrough moment, invented the polymerase chain reaction.

# Beauty in Simplicity

The appropriately named polymerase chain reaction involves a series of cycles, or a chain of reactions, that employ DNA polymerase. The goal of PCR is to amplify, or increase, the concentration of a specific piece of DNA. From information about the sequence of the template DNA, the DNA to be copied, the scientist can design specific oligonucleotides that hybridize only to selected locations on the template. The two oligonucleotides, called *primers* because they prime or initiate the polymerization reaction, must bind to opposite strands of the double-stranded DNA template. Heating breaks the bonds holding together the two strands of the template, causing them to separate. As the sample cools, the primers hybridize to the specifically chosen sites on the new single-stranded template DNA. DNA polymerase then extends the primers, adding new nucleotides to them, creating a complementary strand, and completing the first cycle. As the second round begins, the double-stranded DNA that now consists of one original strand and one newly synthesized strand is heated, so that the two strands separate in a process called denaturation. As the temperature decreases, new primers bind to complementary DNA on both the original and the newly synthesized strands. Again, DNA polymerase extends the primers, creating new double-stranded molecules of DNA. By the end of 20 cycles, the amount of DNA theoretically has increased by 1 million times ($2^{20} = 1,048,576$), and by 30 cycles, 1 billion times ($2^{30} = 1,073,741,824$).

Mullis had come up with a way to provide an experimenter with an unlimited supply of any specific DNA. He was so excited he had to pull over twice on his drive to Mendocino. The concept seemed so simple that he felt sure someone else already must have attempted it. He spent the following Monday searching the Cetus library for some evidence that his scheme was not original, or for some reason why it might not work. Finding neither, he proceeded to ask his molecular biological friends for their opinions, but the idea still seemed sound. Throughout the summer, he continued to talk publicly about PCR and even gave a seminar on the subject at Cetus, but the reception was indifferent. Mullis was apparently the only one capable of foreseeing the future success and potential utility of this procedure.

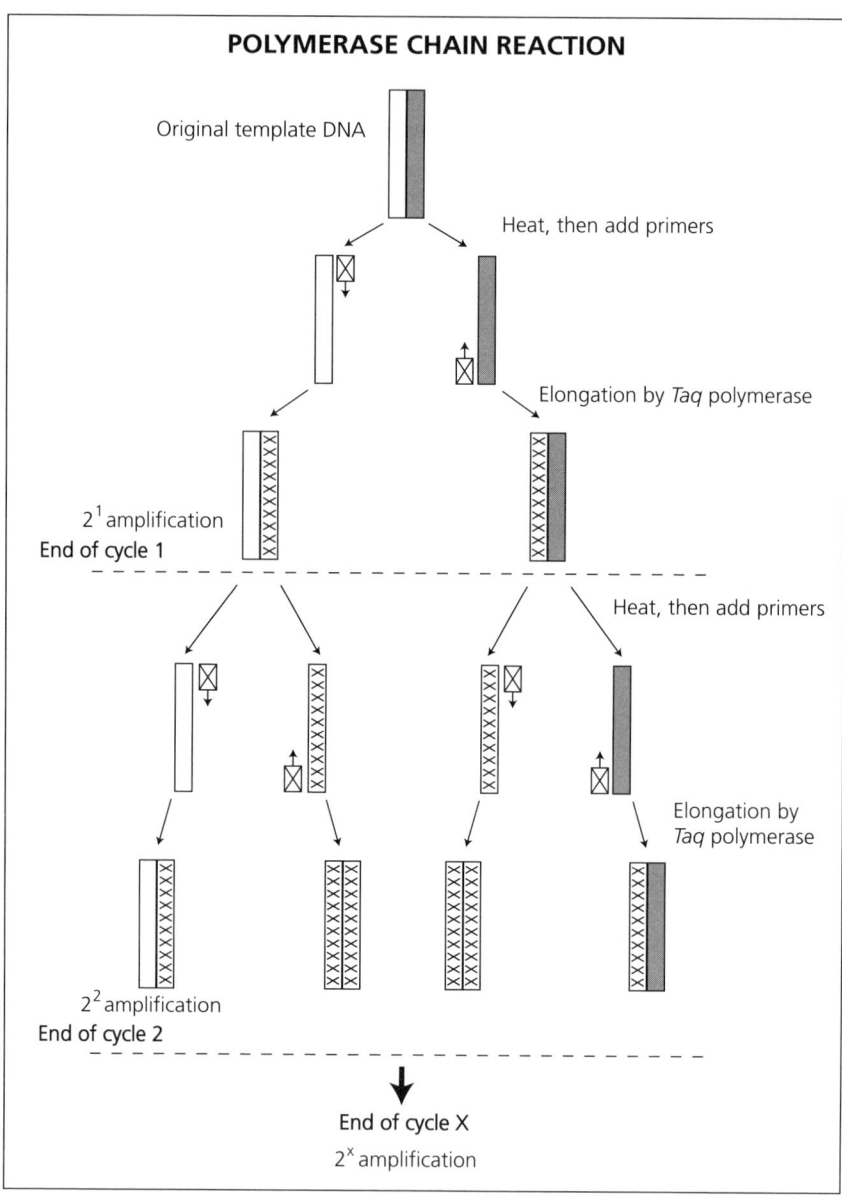

The polymerase chain reaction is a common laboratory procedure used to amplify DNA exponentially.

Perhaps Mullis was discouraged, or maybe just preoccupied, but he did not perform his first experimental attempt at PCR until that September. For his target DNA, he chose a 400-base pair fragment from the human nerve growth factor gene, a single copy gene within the human genome, and designed the appropriate primers. He combined human DNA with the nerve growth factor primers in a small tube, boiled the mixture to denature the DNA, cooled it, added DNA polymerase, and left it sitting at 98.6°F (37°C) overnight. The next day, he anxiously looked for a 400-base pair fragment using a procedure called gel electrophoresis and a stain that causes DNA to fluoresce when exposed to ultraviolet radiation. He saw nothing but was not very surprised. The rate for dissociation of the two strands of DNA was too slow, meaning he would have to heat the tube after each cycle in order to denature the DNA. Because high temperatures destroy DNA polymerase, fresh enzyme would have to be added after every denaturation event. The procedure was going to be a lot more time-consuming than Mullis originally anticipated. He spent three months making several modifications to the reagent concentrations and the temperatures and lengths of incubations, and he even changed the target DNA to a region of a plasmid. (Plasmids are closed, circular DNA molecules found in some bacteria.) His persistence paid off, and on December 16, 1983, Mullis amplified a short fragment of DNA by PCR.

He continued to work on improving his technique. By June 1984, Mullis was at risk of losing his job at Cetus due to his perceived inability to work as part of a multidisciplinary project team. The personnel department gave Mullis one probationary year to prove the merits of PCR. Though Mullis believed he already had demonstrated success, his peers required further proof, including better controls and more complete experiments. By that November, experiments clearly showed PCR worked, and skilled technicians refined the conditions until they obtained reliable, quantitative data showing amplification of DNA hundreds of thousands of times. Cetus filed the first PCR patent on March 28, 1985.

## Gradual Acknowledgment

Though this accomplishment soon would revolutionize biotechnological research, remarkably, the prestigious scientific journals *Nature* and *Science* both rejected its publication, calling the paper

> ## A Stable Enzyme
>
> After inventing PCR technology in 1983, Mullis anticipated the need for a thermostable DNA polymerase to automate and popularize the method. The use of a heat-stable polymerase would prevent researchers from having to add fresh enzyme after the denaturation step of every cycle. In 1986, David Gelfand and Susanne Stoffel of Cetus purified *Taq* polymerase, the DNA polymerase from *Thermus aquaticus*. *T. aquaticus* is a thermophilic (heat-loving), rod-shaped, prokaryotic organism that bacteriologist Thomas D. Brock first isolated from hot springs in the Great Fountain area of the Lower Geyser Basin of Yellowstone National Park in the late 1960s. The organism grows at temperatures between 122°F and 176°F (50–80°C), and its enzymes function optimally around 158°F (70°C) but can withstand heating up to 203°F

too technical and unoriginal. Mullis finally did publish his description of PCR in *Methods in Enzymology* in 1987 under the title "Specific Synthesis of DNA in Vitro via a Polymerase-Catalyzed Chain Reaction." In December 1985, *Science* had published the first application paper, "Enzymatic Amplification of Beta-Globin Genomic Sequences and Restriction Site Analysis for Diagnosis of Sickle Cell Anemia," with Mullis listed as the third of seven coauthors. Mullis presented PCR at a Cold Spring Harbor symposium in May of 1986, and his talk, "Specific Enzymatic Amplification of DNA in Vitro: The Polymerase Chain Reaction," was published in the symposium's proceedings.

The Royal Swedish Academy of Sciences awarded Mullis the Nobel Prize in chemistry for 1993, shared with Michael Smith (1932–2000), "for their contributions to the developments of methods within DNA-based chemistry." Smith was a Canadian molecular biologist from the University of British Columbia who

(95°C), the temperature at which denaturation usually is performed during PCR. The discovery of organisms that lived in such extreme environments was remarkable because high temperatures destroy most biological molecules such as proteins and DNA. *T. aquaticus* was so unique compared with known organisms, that its discovery led to the proposal of a new, third domain of life, the Archaea, characterized by prokaryotic organisms that live in extreme conditions such as those that likely existed on the primitive Earth, and therefore provide insight into the origin of life. (The other two domains of life are Bacteria and Eukarya.)

Brock was not searching for a commercially beneficial microbial product, but his finding demonstrated the usefulness of undirected basic research. Gelfand, Stoffel, and others received the patent for purified *Taq* polymerase in 1989, the same year that *Science,* one of the journals that had rejected Mullis's original paper describing PCR only three years earlier, named the enzyme "Molecule of the Year." Today, most PCR is performed using cheaply produced, cloned, recombinant *Taq* polymerase.

developed the technique of oligonucleotide-based, site-directed mutagenesis of DNA. The rapid awarding of the Nobel Prize for something discovered less than a decade before was testament to the profound impact PCR had on scientific research. That same year, Mullis received the prestigious Japan Prize for his invention of PCR.

Cetus became involved in a battle with E. I. Dupont de Nemours and Company over rights to the patent for PCR. Cetus eventually won but later sold the patent to Hoffmann-La Roche for $300 million. Mullis was rewarded for his contributions with a check for $10,000, the largest bonus Cetus ever had paid to a scientist. Mullis left Cetus in 1986, and Xytronyx, in San Diego, hired him as director of molecular biology. He worked on DNA technology and photochemistry for a while, and in 1987 he began consulting privately on nucleic acid chemistry for numerous corporations, making it his full-time occupation in 1988. Mullis had always wanted to write, and he successfully completed his first book in 1998, when he published *Dancing Naked in the Mind Field*, an autobiographical exploration of his thoughts and opinions on a variety of subjects, including modern science, the use of hallucinogenic drugs, the workings of large companies, and romantic relationships. That same year, Mullis married his fourth wife, Nancy Lier Cosgrove, with whom he lives in Newport Beach, California, and in Anderson Valley, California. He was a director emeritus for Burstein Technologies in Irvine and recently founded Altermune, LLC, a venture resulting from his newest patent on chemically programmable immunity.

## Positive and Negative Publicity

Modifications to the technique of PCR improved its efficiency, reliability, and versatility, and as Mullis predicted, its use spread like wildfire. As a result, the discoverer was inundated with numerous awards in the early 1990s, including the National Biotechnology Award (1991), the R&D Scientist of the Year Award (1991), the California Scientist of the Year Award (1992), the Thomas A. Edison Award (1993), and many more. He also received an honorary doctorate degree from the University of South Carolina in 1994 and was inducted into the National Inventors Hall of Fame in 1998.

Not everyone agreed that Mullis deserved so much recognition; in fact, several of his scientific colleagues resented that fact that Mullis received so much publicity, much less the coveted Nobel Prize. As a confessed psychedelic drug-using surfer, he was not an ideal poster boy for science, and he had a reputation for creating unwanted controversy. Mullis declared that the human immunodeficiency virus (HIV) did not cause acquired immune deficiency syndrome (AIDS), despite the fact that this theory was widely accepted by the medical community. He also argued that the ozone layer was intact, opposing the findings of reputed atmospheric scientists. He even declared that he had an experience with extraterrestrials, asserted that his dead grandfather once spent several days visiting him, and affirmed astrological claims.

Even if many of Mullis's outlandish beliefs seem silly, the benefits of the procedure he imagined and first performed cannot be denied.

The isolation and characterization of the heat-stable *Taq* DNA polymerase and the development of automated temperature cycling machines reduced effort to a minimum; a researcher can set up a PCR reaction in only a few minutes and return within a couple of hours to retrieve the amplified samples. The versatile procedure of PCR is used to diagnose genetic disorders, identify infectious disease agents, determine paternity, perform forensic analyses, and relate extinct organisms with extant life forms. From a dried-up, tiny drop of blood evidence on the upholstery inside of a car to a bit of pulp extracted from a tooth belonging to the mummified remains of ancient royalty, the amazing feat of PCR can garner useful information from a single molecule of DNA. Because all molecular laboratories employ PCR as a standard procedure within their modern research programs, laboratory researchers no longer marvel at the convenience of plentiful supplies of specific DNA afforded by PCR. Mullis's momentous innovation transformed biotechnology by giving scientists an invaluable means to manipulate genetic material.

## CHRONOLOGY

| | |
|---|---|
| 1944 | Kary Mullis is born on December 28 in Lenoir, North Carolina |
| 1966 | Receives a bachelor of science degree in chemistry from the Georgia Institute of Technology |
| 1972 | Earns a Ph.D. in biochemistry from the University of California at Berkeley and lectures in biochemistry |
| 1973 | Begins researching lung disease as a postdoctoral fellow in pediatric cardiology at the University of Kansas Medical School |
| 1977–79 | Studies pharmaceutical chemistry at the University of California at San Francisco |
| 1979–86 | Researches oligonucleotide synthesis as a DNA chemist at the Cetus Corporation in Emeryville, California |
| 1983 | Conceptualizes the process of the polymerase chain reaction |
| 1984 | Clearly demonstrates amplification of DNA by PCR |

| | |
|---|---|
| 1986 | Becomes director of molecular biology at Xytronyx, Inc., in San Diego, and focuses on DNA technology and photochemistry |
| 1987 | Publishes a paper describing the fundamentals of PCR and begins privately consulting on nucleic acid chemistry for corporations |
| 1993 | Shares Nobel Prize in chemistry with Michael Smith for contributions to the developments of methods within DNA-based chemistry. Also receives the Japan Prize for his invention of PCR |
| 1998 | Publishes *Dancing Naked in the Mind Field* |

## FURTHER READING

KaryMullis.com. Available online. URL: http://www.karymullis.com. Accessed on March 8, 2005. Mullis's personal Web site, containing links to information about PCR, his Nobel Prize, his thoughts on science, and more.

Mullis, Kary B. *Dancing Naked in the Mind Field.* New York: Pantheon Books, 1998. Humorous, brief essays on a wide range of subjects including PCR, working in a laboratory, and the scientific method.

———. "The Unusual Origin of the Polymerase Chain Reaction," *Scientific American* 262, no. 4 (1990): 56–65. Mullis's description of the momentous occasion when he conceptualized PCR while driving in California.

Nobelprize.org. "The Nobel Prize in Chemistry 1993." Available online. URL: http://www.nobelprize.org/chemistry/laureates/1993. Last modified on November 1, 2000. Contains links to an illustrated presentation and the autobiographies and Nobel lectures of Mullis and Smith.

Rabinow, Paul. *Making PCR: A Story of Biotechnology.* Chicago: University of Chicago Press, 1996. A behind-the-scenes account of the invention of PCR, including interviews with many of the people involved.

# 10

# Ian Wilmut

## (1944– )

Ian Wilmut led a team of researchers that cloned the first mammal from an adult cell. (James King-Holmes/ Science Photo Library/Photo Researchers, Inc.)

## The First Cloned Mammal

The term *clone* can refer to any object that is a copy of an original; one may purchase a cheaper clone of a popular computer, or a fleet of airplanes may be clones of a previous design. In the biological sense, to clone means to reproduce asexually, or to give rise to genetically identical cells or organisms. In 1938, German biologist Hans Spemann proposed removing the nucleus from an unfertilized egg and replacing it with the nucleus from a *differentiated* (specialized) cell, a process called nuclear transfer (NT). Only 14 years later, scientists began these experiments, first using very early embryonic cells as the donors, then cells from progressively later stages of development. Because scientists performed this work using amphibians rather than mammals, society was apathetic about these achievements. By the early 1980s, successful NT was reported in mice, but the results were not reproducible, and the integrity of the researchers was called into question. In 1984, after numerous painstaking attempts at NT, American embryologist James McGrath and his German colleague Davor Solter emphatically declared that mammalian cloning by NT was impossible. Most scientists agreed, but they were wrong. Danish veterinarian Steen Willadsen reported cloning a lamb from an embryonic sheep cell using NT in 1986. Others soon followed this first verified instance of a cloned mammal. Continued research led to the 1994 cloning of calves from embryos that had reached the 120-cell stage by Neal First at the University of Wisconsin. This was the state of the field when British embryologist Ian Wilmut led a team of researchers at Roslin Institute in Edinburgh, Scotland, to clone sheep first from embryonic cells and then from a six-year-old adult. The 1986 live birth of Dolly, the first mammal cloned from an adult cell, was a remarkable biotechnological breakthrough, but just as significantly, the event brought the potential of human cloning to light.

## The Development of an Interest in Development

Ian Wilmut was born on July 7, 1944, in Hampton Lucey, England. His father, David Wilmut, was a math teacher and his mother, a housewife. As a child growing up in Coventry, Ian wanted to enter the navy, but he was color-blind, a condition that would have prevented his being able to read signals from other boats. He was interested in the outdoors, and though he lived in an industrial area, as a teenager, he worked on farms during the weekends. He especially enjoyed working with the animals; performing tasks such as milking cows and assisting during births instilled in Ian a desire to study farming.

Wilmut attended the University of Nottingham and spent the summer of 1966 as an intern in the laboratory of Professor E. J. Chris Polge in the unit of reproductive physiology and biochemistry at the University of Cambridge. At the time, Polge was trying to understand how an animal knew whether she was pregnant, so her body could make the physiological decision of preparing to mate again or to focus on maintaining the pregnancy. Wilmut became fascinated with embryos and the fact that entire organisms developed from a single cell, an experience that caused Wilmut's interests to shift from practical agriculture to embryological research. He received a bachelor of science degree in animal physiology from Nottingham in 1967.

After marrying his high school sweetheart, Vivienne, with whom he has three grown children, Wilmut entered graduate school at the University of Cambridge. Back in Polge's laboratory, Wilmut examined the reasons bull semen could survive freezing and thawing but boar semen could not. In 1971, Wilmut obtained a doctorate degree in animal engineering from the University of Cambridge. His dissertation was titled "Deep Freeze Preservation of Boar Semen." After completing his Ph.D., Wilmut received a postdoctoral fellowship to stay at Cambridge and continue his freezing research. His goal was to develop deep-freeze storage methods for mammalian embryos. He became the first scientist to freeze a calf embryo, thaw it, and grow it inside a surrogate mother. A live birth resulted in a healthy calf named Frostie, an exciting event because until then, *cryopreservation*, the procedure of freezing cells or embryos for later use, had only been applied to single cells. The development of this technique led to better quality herds because farmers could implant embryos from genetically superior parents into inferior cows.

In 1973, the Animal Breeding Organization (ABRO) in Scotland hired Wilmut, now considered an expert in reproductive physiology, as an embryologist. Later renamed Roslin Institute, the animal genetics research center that was funded by a combination of government and private funds expanded, and Wilmut became one of its leading scientists. In 1981, he was promoted to principal investigator in animal physiology and genetics, in 1993, to principal investigator and joint head of the department of gene expression and development, and then in 2000, head of the department of gene expression and development. His research initially focused on the identification of developmental and physiological causes of embryo death in farm animals, but the interests of ABRO changed toward molecular biology in the early 1980s. At the time, Wilmut resented being told to discontinue his research in progress and to redirect his efforts to the genetic modification of sheep, but he obliged his director, mostly because he and his wife did not want to uproot their family.

Wilmut spent much of the next decade preparing zygotes (the one-celled fusion products of eggs and sperm) for injection with human genes that encoded pharmaceutically important proteins, a project supported by a collaborating biotech company called PPL. After injection, he placed the zygotes back into a ewe and hoped the offspring would express the special gene. A major disadvantage of this method for genetically modifying animals is that each attempt with a single zygote demanded an entire animal. He did succeed in producing Tracy, born in 1990, a sheep that carried the gene encoding alpha-1-antitrypsin, a protein used to treat cystic fibrosis and emphysema, and secreted the human protein in her milk.

## The Unplanned Path to Dolly

Many plants can reproduce asexually by vegetative propagation, a procedure in which a horticulturist trims a section of a root or stem from a plant and it grows into a mature plant that is genetically identical to the donor. This characteristic is beneficial to farmers, who have an economic interest in propagating potatoes that have a particularly smooth texture or flowers that have uniquely decorated petals. The ability to create replicates of farm animals with favorable characteristics was a practical goal of agriculture in the 1980s—to create multiple animals from a genetically superior dairy cow that produced a high yield of milk, for example. One often cannot measure the success of a selective breeding until the offspring reach adulthood, an expensive venture when unsuccessful. Previous failed attempts convinced many scientists that cloning large farm animals was not feasible.

In the early 1980s, Steen Willadsen (1944– ), a Danish researcher from Polge's laboratory, had the best track record for attempts leading to cloning a mammal from differentiated cells, cells that have begun the processes leading to specialization. He developed methods for separating cells from cattle and sheep embryos at the eight-cell stage and nurturing them to adulthood. During the 1983–84 breeding season, he succeeded in fusing a sheep cell from an eight-cell embryo with an enucleated egg cell (a cell whose nucleus has been removed), producing the first cloned farm animal. Willadsen did not publish these results until 1986 ("Nuclear Transplantation of Sheep Embryos," in *Nature*). In 1985, Willadsen left Cambridge and took a job with Grenada Genetics in Texas, where he proceeded to clone a cow from a one-week-old differentiated embryonic cell using NT. At a pub in Dublin, Ireland, in January 1987, Wilmut heard about Willadsen's progress in developing the method of NT using early embryonic cells, and he became convinced that he could genetically modify sheep using transformed embryonic stem (ES) cells. ES cells are the cells from which an entire organism develops and that have the capacity to develop into any different tissue type, such as bone, nerve, or muscle.

Wilmut thought their success rate in genetically modifying sheep would increase if they added DNA to a whole plate of cultured cells and only created embryos from ones that incorporated the DNA, but cultured cells did not develop into whole animals. Researchers were able to culture mouse ES cells, genetically modify them, and put them back into embryos that developed into live births. Providence sometimes directed the altered ES cells to differentiate into gamete-producing cells, creating new genetic strains. Wilmut wanted to create ES cell lines from sheep, but culturing the cells destroyed their ability to develop into different types of specialized tissues.

Keith Campbell (1954– ), a cell biologist with expertise in the cell cycle, joined Wilmut in 1991 at ABRO to assist in the quest to produce genetically modified sheep. Preliminary efforts to make

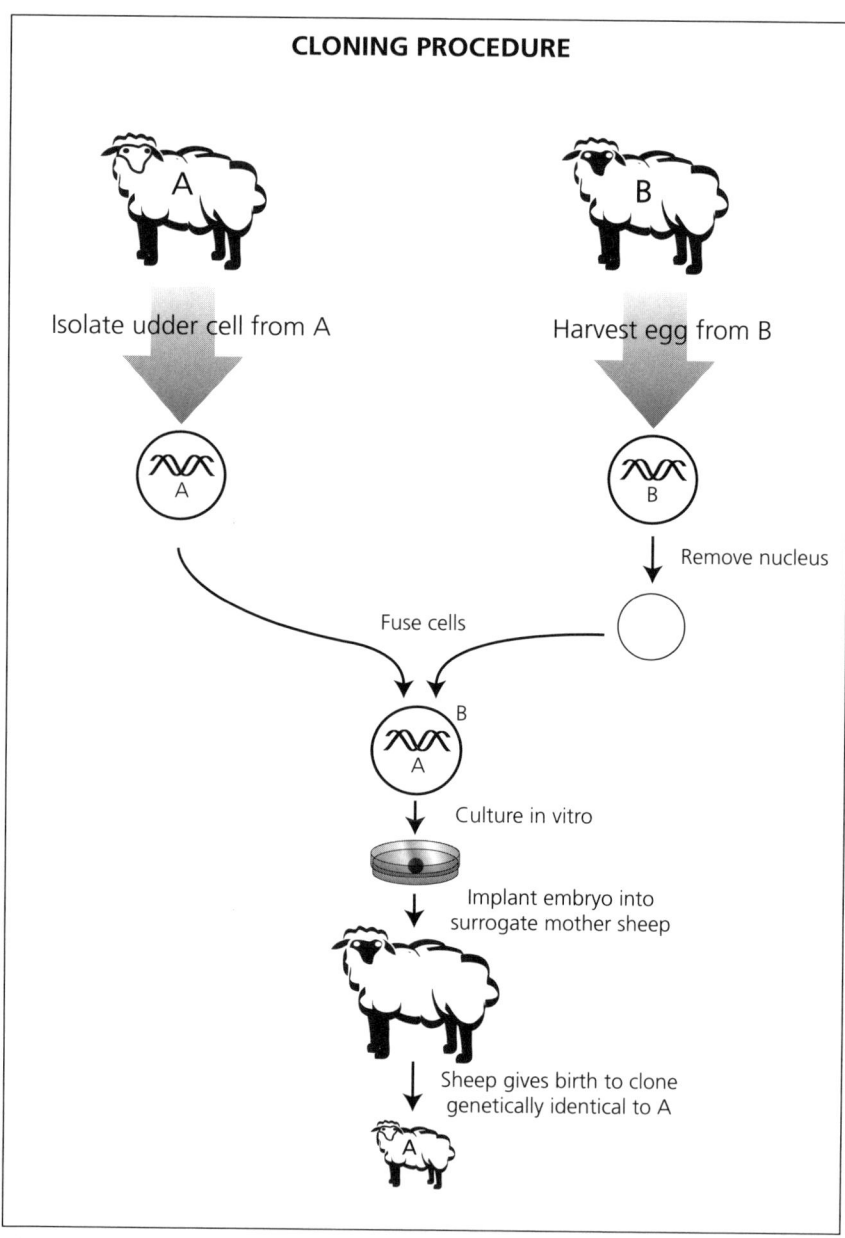

Cloning consists of removing the nucleus from an unfertilized recipient egg, fusing the donor cell with the enucleated egg by electrical stimulation, culturing the cloned embryo in the laboratory (this can also be done in the oviducts of a ewe), and transferring the developing embryo into the reproductive tract of a surrogate mother.

undifferentiated sheep cell lines from cultured ES cells were futile. The cells grew in vitro, but they continued to differentiate. Despite this, Wilmut and Campbell attempted to force the cells into a state of resting or inactivity, called *quiescence*, by starving them. Active embryonic cells normally cycle between growing and dividing, but nutrient deprivation can induce quiescence. They outlined a method of starving cells in order to coordinate the cycle of the cell containing the donor nucleus and the egg cell to which the donor cell is fused. After synchronizing the cultured ES cell nuclear donor and unfertilized recipient sheep egg cells, they attempted to transfer nuclei by fusing the enucleated cell and the egg cell using blasts of electrical current.

Of 244 nuclear transfers that Wilmut and Campbell performed using nine-day-old cultured embryo cells, 34 developed enough to be transferred to the uteri of surrogate mother sheep. In 1995, five lambs were born, including Megan and Morag, the first two mammals cloned from cultured differentiated cells that survived to become healthy, fertile adults. Wilmut views these sheep as the most important of all their clones, since they were the first clones created from frozen cultured cells.

In 1996, they repeated their experiments using nine-day-old embryonic cells that they transferred into eggs from which the genetic material had been removed. Feeling more propitious this time, they also used cultured 26-day-old fetal fibroblast cells and mammary gland cells that had been removed from a six-year-old ewe, cultured in vitro, and frozen in liquid nitrogen. Of 835 total attempts, ultrasound revealed 21 single fetuses that led to eight live births. Of the 277 attempts using mammary cells, Wilmut and Campbell transferred 29 embryos into surrogate mother sheep, resulting in a single live birth. The lamb, named Dolly (after country-music singer Dolly Parton), born on July 5, 1996, resulted from the nuclear transfer of adult cells. Though Dolly was clearly a Finn Dorset ewe, as opposed to progeny of the Scottish blackface ewe that supplied the enucleated egg, DNA testing definitively proved Dolly was indeed a clone. Wilmut and Campbell attributed their success to the exact attention they paid to synchronizing the cell cycles of the donor and recipient cells.

## A Frenzied Response

Roslin Institute did not announce their results until 1997 in order to be sure that Dolly was healthy and developing normally. Their *Nature* article, "Viable Offspring Derived from Fetal and Adult Mammalian Cells," grabbed the attention of the entire world. The media had a field day, emphasizing the closeness to human cloning represented by Dolly, as the first mammal cloned from adult cells. The number of requests for television, radio, and print media interviews far exceeded the expectations of Wilmut, who did not anticipate the controversy the announcement would cause. He never intended to clone human beings, and the thought disgusted him.

### Reproductive v. Therapeutic Cloning in Humans

Fueled by the birth of Dolly, U.S. lawmakers have struggled to reach an agreement on cloning legislation. This is largely due to persistent differences in opinion regarding ethical issues raised by different types of cloning. Some groups feel all cloning should be prohibited, while others feel therapeutic cloning is acceptable but reproductive cloning is not.

In reproductive cloning, following NT, a physician places the clonal human embryo inside the uterus of a surrogate mother. If implantation occurs, the pregnancy could result in the live birth of a human child that is genetically identical to the donor. The failure rate for animal cloning is high, and many cloned animals that do survive have had genetic anomalies due to abnormal expression or die prematurely from infections or other complications, making opposition to this type of human cloning widespread. The United Nations has begun discussions for a global ban on human reproductive cloning.

He emphasized that no cause of infertility could be cured only by cloning—there was no clinical justification for it. Knowing that some people currently are attempting human reproductive cloning, and that others also will try, bothers Wilmut.

Though Dolly was the culmination of years of gradually increasingly successful experiments performed by numerous researchers, the publicity that Dolly generated made it seem as if scientists secretly had been performing cloning experiments and that this success came unexpectedly. This was far from the truth; every year scientific journals contained numerous articles reporting the successes in developmental biology that led to cloning. Not everyone was pleased with science's latest feat, however, and groups

> The goal of therapeutic cloning is not to produce a child but to harvest stem cells from the clonal embryo. *Embryonic stem cells* are undifferentiated cells that have the capacity to develop into virtually any cell type. They are harvested at five days and can be used to learn about human development and possibly to treat disease. Researchers believe that stem cell research provides the best hope for treating conditions that are presently incurable, such as spinal cord injuries, type I diabetes, and Parkinson's disease.
>
> On August 9, 2001, President George W. Bush announced that federal funds could not be used to create human embryonic stem cells, but no federal law exists that prohibits private funding of stem cell research. In February 2004, South Korean researchers announced the successful cloning of a human embryo as a source of stem cells. In October 2004, researchers at Harvard University began seeking permission to create human stem cells for therapeutic purposes. Also that October, scientists at the University of Chicago announced success in transforming adult stem cells obtained from bone marrow into a specialized type of immune system cell that can produce antibodies.

expressed disapproval in a variety of ways. Nobody went so far as to burn down Wilmut's labs, as animal activists had in 1991, but on March 4, 1997, President Bill Clinton requested a five-year halt on human cloning research and asked the National Bioethics Advisory Commission to review the possibility of human cloning and make recommendations regarding any preventative legal action. Despite a few waves of activity in the U.S. Congress to legislate cloning, no federal statutes exist, leaving the matter up to individual states. As of 2004, only 10 states have laws concerning human cloning, some only banning cloning as a means to reproduce; others ban cloning for research purposes or for therapeutic use in treating degenerative conditions.

# After Dolly

The year after Dolly was born, Roslin achieved another breakthrough, cloning a genetically modified sheep. Wilmut had inserted a gene for the production of a blood clotting factor, protein factor IX, into the nuclear genome of the donor nucleus while it was in culture. The protein was secreted in milk produced by the new sheep, named Polly. Wilmut hopes that similar cloning technology will help make pig organs that could be transplanted into humans, a process called xenotransplantation. Many questions remain unanswered, such as how do cells become differentiated? What factors are important in genetically programming a cell to become specialized? Why is the failure rate of cloning by nuclear transfer so high? What role does cytoplasmic DNA from the recipient play in development?

Dolly gave birth to six offspring, all bred conventionally and apparently healthy. In 2003, examinations showed that the six-year-old Dolly had developed a progressive lung disease, and the decision was made to euthanize her. Sheep normally live 11 or 12 years, and lung disease is common as they age. The year before, veterinarians had diagnosed Dolly with arthritis, sparking a debate on the true age of the first cloned mammal, further fueled by the diagnosis of lung disease at such a young age. The cell from which Dolly was cloned was already six years old before Dolly was born.

Examination of her body after death showed no abnormalities other than arthritis and lung disease.

Since Dolly, others have achieved success cloning cattle, goats, pigs, deer, mules, and mice, but the mortality rate is very high—more than 97 percent die before birth. Some species, such as monkeys, horses, and dogs, are more resistant to cloning than other species for unknown reasons. Cloning technology has been used in a variety of ways, some more controversial than others. In 2000, Japanese scientists recloned a bull, that is, they cloned a baby bull from an adult bull that was itself a clone, testing the limits of science and technology. The following year, European scientists cloned a type of endangered wild sheep called a mouflon. Using reproductive cloning as a means to prevent the extinction of endangered species is an application of the technology that is difficult to fault. More controversial applications of animal cloning include the cloning of a pet house cat by scientists from Texas A&M and the potential cloning of extinct species, a possibility that is very exciting to paleobiologists.

## Many Hopes

In addition to working at Roslin Institute, Wilmut currently serves as scientific adviser of Geron Bio-Med Ltd., a subsidiary of Geron Corporation, a pharmaceutical company that is exploring the biomedical applications of the human embryonic stem cell technology, in other words, therapeutic cloning. Wilmut has served as an editor for the *Journal of Reproduction and Fertility* and is currently the editor in chief for *Cloning and Stem Cells*. In 2000, he copublished *The Second Creation: Dolly and the Age of Biological Control*, with Keith Campbell and Colin Tudge. The authors describe the work leading up to the birth of Dolly and the initial impressions afterward, in addition to trying to dispel some of the myths surrounding Dolly's cloning. On a personal note, Wilmut remains a committed family man who enjoys curling and has run two marathons.

Wilmut's awards and honors include at least three honorary doctorate degrees, the Sir John Hammond Memorial Prize from the Society for the Study of Fertility (1998), the Research Medal from the Royal Agricultural Society of England (1999), the Sir William Young Award from the Royal Highland and Agricultural Society of Scotland (1999), and the Scotsman Innovator of the Year Award, Edinburgh (2001). The Royal Society of Edinburgh elected Wilmut to membership in 2000 and the Royal Society of London in 2002.

Wilmut's accomplishment of cloning a mammal from an adult body cell resulted from a combination of breakthrough technologies in genetic engineering and in cloning methods from cultured cells. The procedure itself is simple to describe, yet took mounds of effort to achieve success and required scientific expertise in embryology and cell biology. Scientists had strongly asserted that mammalian cloning was far-fetched, calling it science fiction, but Wilmut shattered that notion. Society responded strongly because, for the first time, people recognized the eventual possibility of human cloning and were forced to confront the accompanying ethical issues. By cloning a mammal from fully differentiated adult cells, Wilmut and his team answered a basic question of developmental biology, demonstrating that genetic material is not altered irreversibly during differentiation and development. The DNA from specialized cells can be reprogrammed to create an entire new being. Someday scientists might be able to re-create whole, compatible organs from a healthy cell of someone needing a transplant or to replace cells that have been destroyed by degenerative diseases such as Alzheimer's. Scientists dedicated to cloning research have decades of work ahead—so many challenges remain, but so do many hopes.

## CHRONOLOGY

| | |
|---|---|
| 1944 | Ian Wilmut is born on July 7 in Hampton Lucey, England |
| 1967 | Earns a bachelor of science degree in animal physiology from the University of Nottingham |
| 1971 | Receives a doctorate degree in animal genetic engineering from Cambridge University and obtains a postdoctoral fellowship to continue research on cryopreservation of semen and embryos |

| | |
|---|---|
| 1973 | Wilmut's research leads to the first calf born from a frozen embryo. Joins ABRO (later called Roslin Institute) as a senior scientific officer working on embryology |
| 1981 | Is promoted to principal investigator in animal physiology and genetics at Roslin Institute |
| 1982 | Begins researching methods for genetic modification of sheep |
| 1984 | Steen Willadsen clones a sheep from an eight-cell embryo by NT |
| 1985 | Willadsen clones a cow from a differentiated embryonic cell |
| 1987 | Wilmut hears rumors about Willadsen's experiments and becomes convinced that cloning large farm animals is possible |
| 1990 | Tracy, a transgenic sheep that Wilmut modified to produce a human protein, is born |
| 1991 | Keith Campbell joins Wilmut at ABRO |
| 1993 | Wilmut becomes principal investigator and joint head of the department of gene expression and development at Scotland's Roslin Institute |
| 1995 | Clones two sheep, Megan and Morag, from differentiated frozen cells |
| 1996 | Clones a sheep named Dolly, the first mammal cloned from an adult cell |
| 1997 | Publishes announcement of Dolly's birth. Polly, a sheep Wilmut cloned from fetal skin cells and genetically engineered to secrete human protein factor IX in milk, is born |
| 2000 | Becomes head of the department of gene expression and development at Roslin Institute. Cowrites *The Second Creation: Dolly and the Age of Biological Control* with Keith Campbell and Colin Tudge |

## FURTHER READING

Amato, Ivan, ed. *Science Pathways of Discovery.* New York: John Wiley, 2002. Contains essays written by one dozen accomplished scientists, including one about cloning.

*Encyclopedia of World Biography, Supplement.* Vol. 20, 2nd ed. Farmington Hills, Mich.: Gale Group, 2000. Brief biographies of notable figures and summaries of their accomplishments. Written for high school students.

"Human Genome Project Information: Cloning Fact Sheet." U.S. Department of Energy, Office of Science. Available online. URL: http://www.ornl.gov/sci/techresources/Human_Genome/elsi/cloning.shtml#whatis. Last modified on July 9, 2004. Describes general information, news, ethics, legislation, and problems related to cloning. Also contains numerous links to reputable sites for more information on aspects of cloning.

"Ian Wilmut, Ph.D." Academy of Achievement, 2005. Available online. URL: http://www.achievement.org/autodoc/page/wil0bio-1. Last revised on February 5, 2005. Contains a brief biography with a link to an insightful personal interview with Wilmut.

McGee, Glenn, ed. *The Human Cloning Debate.* Berkeley, Calif.: Berkeley Hills Books, 2002. Commentaries written by bioethicists and scientists, including Wilmut, on the pros and cons of cloning, with a good introductory review.

Wilmut, Ian, Keith Campbell, and Colin Tudge. *The Second Creation: Dolly and the Age of Biological Control.* New York: Farrar, Straus, and Giroux, 2000. An account of the revolutionary breakthrough of cloning from the cell of an adult sheep, told by the scientists responsible.

# GLOSSARY

**alternating current**   an electric current that reverses its direction of flow at regular intervals

**amplify**   to make greater, stronger, larger, or more of something

**anode**   a positively charged electrode; the negative terminal of a battery

**artificial radiation**   radiation made by human activity, such as by inducing fission of a nucleus

**atom**   the smallest particle of an element that retains the composition of the element, consisting of protons and neutrons in a central nucleus surrounded by electrons

**atomic weight**   the averaged weight (mass) of all isotopes of a given element

**bacterium** (plural **bacteria**)   one-celled, microscopic, prokaryotic organism

**blastocyst**   an early embryonic stage in mammals; a hollow ball of cells

**cathode**   a negatively charged electrode; the positive terminal of a battery

**clone**   an individual grown from a single body cell of its parent and genetically identical to it; also, to make an identical copy of something, including an organism or a cell

**coherer**   a device for detecting radio waves consisting of a cylinder filled with metal filings that stick to one another when struck by a radio wave, allowing a current to pass through

**complementary**   in genetics, having the capacity for precise pairing between the nucleotides on two strands of DNA such that the sequence of one strand determines the other

**conservation**  the planned management of a natural resource in order to protect it from being destroyed

**cryopreservation**  the process of freezing something, such as a cell or an embryo, for later use

**crystal**  a solid particle formed by the arrangement of atoms, ions, or molecules into a regular, repeating, characteristic pattern

**deoxyribonucleic acid (DNA)**  the molecule that is the basis for heredity, found in the nucleus of eukaryotic cells

**diabetes**  a disease characterized by the inability to uptake sugar into cells, caused by a deficiency of the hormone insulin that is normally produced by the pancreas

**dichlorodiphenyltrichloroethane (DDT)**  a pesticide developed in the 1940s and later banned from use in the United States

**dideoxynucleotide**  a nucleotide chemically altered so that additional nucleotides cannot be linked to it

**differentiated**  in developmental biology, having undergone the processes that lead to cell specialization, such as the turning on or off of specific genes

**diode**  an electronic device that has two electrodes or terminals and is used especially as a rectifier

**direct current**  a steady electric current flowing only in one direction

**DNA polymerase**  the enzyme responsible for synthesizing new DNA molecules

**doping**  adding impurities to change the conduction properties of a semiconductor

**duct**  a hollow tube through which material flows

**ecology**  the study of the interaction between living organisms and their environment

**ecosystem**  an entire community of living things and their environment

**ectopic**  a pregnancy occurring when an embryo implants somewhere other than the uterus, such as in an oviduct

**electromagnetic wave**  a disturbance of electric or magnetic fields that carries energy through space

**embryonic stem cells**  undifferentiated embryonic cells that have the ability to develop into different types of specialized cells, such as nerve cells or muscle cells

**estrogen** a female steroid hormone that plays an important role in sexual development and reproduction

**fermentation** a chemical process that breaks down organic materials and does not require oxygen

**food chain** the pathway along which food energy is transferred between trophic levels. Plants and small organisms are eaten by larger, stronger organisms, which are, in turn, eaten by still stronger organisms

**frequency** in electronics, the number of complete cycles per second of an alternating current or other wave

**gamete** an egg or sperm cell that can unite with the other during fertilization to form a zygote

**gonadotropin** a hormone that stimulates the activity of the testes or ovaries, such as follicle-stimulating hormone (FSH) or luteinizing hormone (LH)

**gynecologist** a physician who specializes in the care of the female reproductive system

**herbicide** a chemical that destroys unwanted plants or inhibits their growth

**hybridization** in genetics, the process of two complementary strands of DNA coming together by specific pairing between nucleotide bases

**implantation** the attachment of an embryo to the uterine wall in a placental mammal

**infertility** the inability of a male and female to produce offspring together

**insulin** a protein hormone produced in the pancreas that is necessary for sugar uptake by cells

**interdisciplinary** drawing upon knowledge from many disciplines

**in vitro fertilization (IVF)** the fertilization of an egg in a test tube in the laboratory, usually followed by attempts to implant the embryo inside the mother

**ionosphere** the region of the atmosphere that extends between 50 miles (80 km) and 300 miles (483 km) from the Earth's surface and contains layers of ionized gases that facilitate the transmission of radio waves over long distances

**islets of Langerhans** glands in the pancreas that produce insulin

**laparoscopy** an operation that uses a fiber-optic instrument inserted into the abdomen through a small incision in order to examine a patient's interior

**luminescence** the emission of light without heat, such as by a chemical or physiological process

**microbiology** the study of microscopic organisms such as bacteria and protozoa

**molecule** the smallest particle of a substance that retains all the properties of the substance and is composed of one or more atoms

**nucleotide** a building block of DNA. Four different nucleotides (A, C, T, and G) are linked together to produce a single strand of DNA

**obstetrician** a physician who specializes in birth

**oligomer restriction** a method formerly used to identify point mutations in DNA

**oligonucleotide** a short piece of DNA, approximately 20 nucleotides in length

**oscillator** a device that produces an alternating current from a direct current

**ovary** the female gonad; produces female steroid hormones and eggs

**oviducts** the tubes that carry eggs released from the ovaries to the uterus

**pancreas** a long, irregular-shaped gland lying behind the stomach that produces digestive juices and the hormone insulin

**pasteurization** the partial sterilization of a substance, often a liquid, by heating at specific temperatures for certain periods of time, killing pathogenic microbes without chemically altering the substance

**pesticide** any agent used to kill pests such as insects

**plankton** mostly microscopic organisms that live near the surface within a body of water

**plasmid** an extrachromosomal, closed, circular DNA molecule found in some microorganisms

**polonium**   a rare, radioactive chemical element with atomic number 84

**polymerase chain reaction (PCR)**   a biotechnological procedure used to produce relatively large quantities of a specific DNA sequence

**primer**   in genetics, an oligonucleotide used to initiate synthesis of DNA, to which new nucleotides are added

**progesterone**   a female steroid hormone that is necessary for the establishment and maintenance of pregnancy

**quiescence**   a state of resting or inactivity

**radio**   a means of sending and receiving sound by the transmission of electromagnetic waves without wires

**radioactivity**   the spontaneous emission of energetic particles such as alpha rays, beta rays, or gamma rays by the disintegration of their atomic nuclei; also, the rays that are emitted by spontaneous nuclear decay

**radium**   a radioactive element with the atomic number 88 that forms from uranium decay

**receiver**   in electronics, a device that converts electromagnetic radiation into sound or picture

**rectify**   to change an electronic signal from an alternating current to a direct current

**restriction enzyme**   a protein that cuts DNA molecules at a specific sequence

**semiconductor**   a solid that has an intermediate level of conductivity, between that of a conductor and an insulator

**stereochemistry**   the spatial arrangement of atoms within molecules; or the branch of chemistry that deals with the spatial arrangement of atoms within molecules and the properties associated with the arrangement

**sterilization**   in microbiology, to make free of living microorganisms; in medicine, a procedure that makes one incapable of producing offspring

**subatomic particles**   units of matter smaller than atoms, such as protons and electrons

**superovulate**   to produce more than the usual number of mature ova at one time

**template** in genetics, the strand of DNA that polymerase reads in order to determine which nucleotides to add to the strand being synthesized

**transistor** a small crystal device containing semiconductors that controls the flow of an electric current through an electric device

**transmitter** a device that generates radio waves to be sent out through space and picked up by a receiver

**uterus** the female reproductive organ that accommodates the developing embryo and then fetus until birth

**vaccine** an inoculation administered to confer or increase immunity to a specific disease

**vacuum tube** a sealed glass tube from which all the air has been removed

**valence** outermost, as in the outermost electron shell of an atom

**virus** a submicroscopic infectious particle that consists of an outer protein coat surrounding nucleic acid and that depends on a host cell for multiplication

**wavelength** the distance between one peak or crest of a wave and the next

**X-ray** an electromagnetic disturbance such as light but with a much higher frequency

**zoology** the scientific study of the animal kingdom

**zygote** the product resulting from the fusion of a sperm cell and an egg cell

# FURTHER RESOURCES

## Books

Aaseng, Nathan. *Black Inventors.* New York: Facts On File, 1997. Profiles 10 African-American men and women whose inventions have revolutionized technology.

Brockman, John, ed. *The Greatest Inventions of the Past 2,000 Years.* New York: Simon and Schuster, 2000. Answers given by the world's foremost scientists when asked what they believed to be the greatest invention of the past 2,000 years.

Dulken, Stephen Van. *Inventing the 20th Century: 100 Inventions That Shaped the World.* New York: New York University Press, 2000. Brief histories and copies of original patent applications for everyday devices such as the zipper and the Post-It note.

Evans, Harold. *They Made America.* New York: Little, Brown, 2004. Contains short profiles of American innovators, including not only the scientists and inventors, but the businesspeople who brought their innovations to society.

*History of Invention.* 8 vols. New York: Facts On File, 2004. The progress of human technology, outlined in eight volumes, with each one encompassing a broad theme (such as *Communication and Computers* and *Power and Energy*). Written for grades six and up.

*The New Popular Book of Science.* Vol. 6. Danbury, Conn.: Grolier, 2004. An overview of technology from the Stone Age to modern-day genetic engineering at a level appropriate for middle and high school students.

Oakes, Elizabeth H. *A to Z of STS Scientists.* New York: Facts On File, 2002. Profiles more than 150 scientists, discussing their research and contributions. Includes bibliography, cross-references, and chronology.

Rhodes, Richard, ed. *Visions of Technology.* New York: Simon and Schuster, 1999. Views and opinions about the effects of technology on society.

Vare, Ethlie Ann, and Greg Ptacek. *Patently Female: From AZT to TV Dinners, Stories of Women Inventors and Their Breakthrough Ideas.* New York: John Wiley, 2002. Salutes resourceful women whose inventions have changed society.

Volti, Rudi. *The Facts On File Encyclopedia of Science, Technology, and Society.* 3 vols. New York: Facts On File, 1999. Comprehensive reference of 900 entries revealing how economics, society, and culture produce scientific and technological advances.

Yenne, Bill. *100 Inventions That Shaped World History.* San Francisco, Calif.: Bluewood Books, 1993. Brief descriptions and illustrations of the world's most important inventions.

## Internet Resources

Amusement Park Physics. Annenberg/CPB, 2005. Available online. URL: http://www.learner.org/exhibits/parkphysics/coaster.html. Accessed on March 8, 2005. Explains how science is applied to build roller-coasters, carousels, bumper cars, and more.

Bellis, Mary. "Inventors." About, Inc., 2005. Available online. URL: http://inventors.about.com. Accessed on March 8, 2005. Contains regular feature articles. Visit links under "Essentials" to view a time line of 20th-century inventions or to search an alphabetical listing of inventors and inventions. Explore links under "Articles and Resources" for more in-depth information about specific inventors or inventions.

EcoKids. Earth Day Canada, 2003. Available online. URL: http://www.ecokidsonline.com/pub/index.cfm. Accessed on March 8, 2005. Web site for Canada's environmental education program for youths that teaches topical information through interactive games and activities.

Gomez-Romero, Pedro. "Science, Technology, and Society." Available online. URL: http://www.geocities.com/capecanaveral/hangar/9434. Last modified on December 1, 2003. News stories and information on a variety of STS topics.

Greatest Engineering Achievements of the 20th Century. National Academy of Engineering, 2000. Available online. URL: http://www.greatachievements.org. Accessed on March 8, 2005. Explore the 20 top achievements of the 20th century.

Invention Dimension. Massachusetts Institute of Technology/MIT School of Engineering. Available online. URL: http://web.mit.edu/invent/invent-main.html. Accessed on March 8, 2005. Explore the links "Inventor of the Week," "Inventor's Handbook," and "Games and Trivia" for a fun way to learn about inventions.

Invent Now: National Inventors Hall of Fame. National Inventors Hall of Fame, 2005. Available online. URL: http://www.invent.org/hall_of_fame/1_0_0_hall_of_fame.asp. Accessed on March 8, 2005. Search for profiles about the inductees of the Hall of Fame's archives by inventor, invention, or induction date.

Lemelson Center for the Study of Invention and Innovation. Invention at Play. Smithsonian National Museum of American History, Behring Center. Available online. URL: http://www.inventionatplay.org. Accessed on March 8, 2005. An interactive Web site that emphasizes the playful aspect of inventing.

Mikulski, Steve. The Technology Education Lab: Preparing Minds for the 21st Century. The Technology Education Lab, 2005. Available online. URL: http://www.techedlab.com. Accessed on March 8, 2005. A valuable site for technology education, including links to science and math resources, a description of technology education, teaching resources, and more.

Science, Technology, and Society. North Chadderton School, England. Available online. URL: http://www.personal.u-net.com/~nchadd/home.htm. Accessed on March 8, 2005. Contains links for STS resources and discussion topics.

Stanford University Program in Science, Technology, and Society. Leland Stanford Junior University, 2004. Available online. URL: http://www.stanford.edu/group/STS. Last updated on February 23, 2005. In addition to providing information about Stanford's undergraduate degree program in STS, this site includes links to STS programs at other schools and useful information on careers in STS.

United States Patent and Trademark Office Kids' Pages. Available online. URL: http://www.uspto.gov/go/kids/index.html. Accessed on March 8, 2005. Follow link "Bright Lights: 6th–12th" to explore stories of invention, see answers to FAQs, learn trivia about inventions, read about careers in the USPTO, and more.

The Why Files: Science Behind the News. University of Wisconsin–Madison, Board of Regents, 2005. Available online. URL: http://whyfiles.org/index.php. Accessed on March 8, 2005. New files posted every week explaining the science or technology that has made news headlines.

## Periodicals

### *Discover*

Published by Buena Vista Magazines
114 Fifth Avenue
New York, NY 10011
Telephone: (212) 633-4400
www.discover.com

A popular monthly magazine containing easy to understand articles on a variety of scientific topics.

### *Inventor's Digest*

30-31 Union Wharf
Boston, MA 02109
Telephone: (617) 367-4540
www.inventorsdigest.com

Quarterly magazine that features successful inventors and provides information for bringing inventions to market.

### *Popular Science*

P.O. Box 60001
Tampa, FL 33660-0001

Telephone: (800) 289-9399
www.popsci.com
A monthly magazine with articles about cutting-edge science and technology breakthroughs.

## Societies and Organizations

For Inspiration and Recognition of Science and Technology (www.usfirst.org) 200 Bedford Street, Manchester, NH 03101. Telephone: (603) 666-3906

International Association for Science, Technology, and Society (www.nasts.org) c/o Susan M. Blunck, IASTS President, University of Maryland, Baltimore County, 1000 Hilltop Circle, Baltimore, MD 21250. Telephone: (410) 455-2869

Invent Now, The National Inventors Hall of Fame (www.invent.org) 221 South Broadway, Akron, OH 44308-1505. Telephone: (330) 762-4463

# INDEX

*Italic* page numbers indicate illustrations.

## A
AIDS. *See* HIV/AIDS
alcohol 6
alpha particles 29, 74
aluminum 29
Anderson, Carl David 71
anode 103
anthrax 10, 12, 13
antibodies 13
*Apollo 11* xi
Armstrong, Neil xi
aseptic technique 12
assisted reproductive technology (ART) 115–116, 124–125. *See also* in vitro fertilization
atomic weapons xix, 67–68, 71–79, 77, *78*
atomic weight 23
atoms 3, 29

## B
bacteria 6–14
Bailey, Jean Alberta 102
Balard, Antoine-Jérôme 3
Ball, Henrietta 62
Banting, Margaret 50
Banting, Sir Frederick xix, *49*, 49–65
Banting, William 50
Banting, William Robertson 61
Bardeen, John 104–105
Barron, Moses 53
Becquerel, Henry 20
beer 11
beets 6
Best, Charles H. 54, 61
beta decay 74
Bezzi-Scali, Countess Maria Christina 45
Bigo 6

biopharmaceuticals 58, *59*
biotechnology xviii, 58, *59*
blastocyst stage 120–121
Born, Max 69, 74
boron 29
Boyer, Herbert 58
Brattain, Walter H. 104, 105
Braun, Karl Ferdinand 43
Bridgman, Percy 69
Brock, Thomas D. 138–139
bromine 3
Brown, Lesley 123
Brown, Louise Joy 123
Bush, George W. 151

## C
Campbell, Keith 147, 149
cancer xvii, xviii, 26, 27, 29
Capon, Laura 75
carbohydrates 52
carbolic acid 12
carbon dioxide 6
Carson, Maria Frazier McLean 86
Carson, Rachel xix, *85*, 85–99,
Carson, Robert Warden 86
Carter, Jimmy 97
cascade process 71
cathode 103
cathode rays 22
cell phones 33, 34
chicken cholera 12–13
chlamydia 117
cholera 10, 12–13
Clinton, Bill 152
cloning xix–xx, 143–144, 147–153, *148*
clothing industry 9
coherer 38, *39*, 43
Collip, J. B. 58, 61
Communist Party 79–80
computers 111

Cooper, Leon Neil 105
cortex, of brain 51
Cosgrove, Nancy Lier 140
cowpox 12
critical mass 76
cryopreservation 145
crystals 3–5, *5*
Curie, Eve 25, 30
Curie, Irène. *See* Joliot-Curie, Irène
Curie, Marie xix, *19*, 19–31
Curie, Pierre 21, 25
curvature, of Earth 42
cystic fibrosis 146

## D
*Dancing Naked in the Mind Field* (Mullis) 140
data xii
DDT (dichlorodiphenyl trichloroethane) 91–95, *92, 94*
denaturation 135. *See also* DNA; polymerase chain reaction
deuterons 71
diabetes xix, 49–50, 52–60
dideoxynucleotide 133, 134. *See also* DNA; polymerase chain reaction
diode 106–107, *107*
disease 11–12
DNA (deoxyribonucleic acid) 132–137
DNA polymerase 132, 133. *See also* polymerase chain reaction
doping 106
drugs, hallucinogenic 131, 140
Dumas, Jean-Baptiste 3

## E
$E = mc^2$ 67
Earth, curvature of 42

ecology 85–86. *See also* Carson, Rachel
economic considerations xvii–xviii
ectopic pregnancy 122
*Edge of the Sea, The* (Carson) 91
Edison, Thomas A. 103
Edward VII (king of Great Britain) 41
Edwards, Robert G. 118
Ehrenfest, Paul 74
eight-cell stage, of human embryo *121*
Einstein, Albert 67, 79
electromagnetic waves 36–37, *37*
electrometer 23
electrons 36, 71, 105, 106–107
*Elettra* (ship) 45
embryo *121*
emphysema 146
endometriosis 117
endorphins 132
Environmental Protection Agency (EPA) 96–97
enzyme, restriction 133
*Escherichia coli* 58
estrogen 122
*Experiments and Observations on Electricity* (Franklin) 35

**F**
Faraday, Michael 35
farm animals 13–14
Federal Insecticide, Fungicide, and Rodenticide Act (FIFRA) 97
female reproductive tract *119*
fermentation 5–7
Fermi, Enrico 74–75
fermium 75
fertility 115–116, 118–120
fertilization, in vitro. *See* in vitro fertilization
fibrosis 62
First, Neal 144
fission, nuclear 71–72, 72
flasks, swan-necked 8, *8*
Fleming, John A. 103
Flying Universities 21
food chain 93–94, *94*

forensics xix
Franklin, Benjamin 35
Frisch, Otto Robert 75

**G**
gamete intrafallopian transfer 124, 125
gamma radiation 29
Gelfand, David 138
genetic engineering xvii, xix
germanium 105
germs 11–12
Gibson, Cynthia 132
Gilchrist, Joe 59
glucose 49
gonadotropin 120
Groves, Leslie 73, 79
gynecology 117

**H**
Haeckel, Ernst 85
hallucinogenic drugs 131, 140
Harding, Warren 28
Harrison, Katherine Puening 71
Henderson, Velyien 57
Hertz, Heinrich 36, 37
Higgins, Elmer 88
HIV/AIDS 15, 140
hormone therapy 122
Huckins, Olga Owens 91
hybridization 133
hypothesis xii

**I**
immune system 13
in vitro fertilization xix, 119–126
infertility 115–116, 117–118
insects 92–93
insulin 49–50, 52–60
ionosphere 42–43
islets of Langerhans 52–54

**J**
Jameson, Annie 34
Jenner, Edward 12
Johnson, Lyndon B. 80–81
Joliot-Curie, Frédéric 28–29
Joliot-Curie, Irène 22, 24, 27, 28–29
Joslin, Eliot P. 61
Jupille, Jean-Baptiste 14

**K**
Kemp, George Stevens 40
Koch, Robert 10–11, 12
Koch's postulates 11

**L**
lactic acid 6
Langerhans, Paul 52
Langevin, Paul 26
Lanning, Emily I. 109
laparoscopic surgery 117–118
*Laparoscopy in Gynaecology* (Steptoe) 118
Laurent, Marie 4
Lawrence, Ernest 73
Leopold, Aldo 86
leukemia 30
light, speed of 67–68
lipids 52
Lister, Joseph 12
luminescence 22

**M**
Macleod, John James Richard 52, 53, 57, 60
magnesium 29
Maloney, Marie (Missy) 28
Manhattan Project 71–79, 77, *78*
Marconi, Alfonso 34
Marconi, Elettra 45
Marconi, Giuseppe 34, 35
Marconi, Guglielmo xix, *33*, 33–47
Marconi, Luigi 34
Maxwell, James Clerk 36
McCarthyism 80
McGrath, James 144
media xviii
medical applications, of radiation 25–26
Mehring, Jospeh von 52
Meister, Joseph 14, 15
Meitner, Lise 75
microbiology 2
microscope, scanning-tunneling 70
microwaves 45
military applications xviii
milk 6
Miller, Frederick R. 51, 53
Minkowski, Oskar 52
Mitterrand, François 30
molecules 4
Morse, Samuel 34
Morse code 34

# Index

mouthwash 12
Muir, John 85–86
Müller, Paul Hermann 91–92
Mullis, Bernice Alberta Barker 130
Mullis, Cecil Banks 130
Mullis, Kary xix, *129*, 129–142
Mullis, Louise 131
Mullis, Richards 131
Mussolini, Benito 75

## N
Napoleon III 9
NASA xi
neutrons 71, 74
nitrogen 29
Nixon, Richard M. 96
Nobel Prize
   awarded to Carl David Anderson 71
   awarded to Sir Frederick G. Banting 61
   awarded to John Bardeen 104
   awarded to Henry Becquerel 25
   awarded to Walter H. Brattain 104
   awarded to Karl Ferdinand Braun 43
   awarded to Leon Neil Cooper 105
   awarded to Marie Curie 25, 27
   awarded to Pierre Curie 25
   awarded to Frédéric Joliot-Curie 28
   awarded to Irène Joliot-Curie 28
   awarded to Robert Koch 10
   awarded to Guglielmo Marconi 43
   awarded to Paul Hermann Müller 91–92
   awarded to Kary Mullis 129–130, 138
   awarded to Ernest Rutherford 28
   awarded to John Robert Schrieffer 105
   awarded to William Shockley 104
   awarded to Frederick Soddy 28
Noble, E. C. 58
nuclear fission 71–72, *72*
nuclear weapons. *See* atomic weapons
nucleotides 132. *See also* DNA

## O
O'Brien, Beatrice 43
obstetrics 117
oligomer restriction assay 133
oligonucleotides 132, 133–134
Oppenheimer, Ella Freedman 68
Oppenheimer, Frank 68
Oppenheimer, J. Robert xix, *67*, 67–82
Oppenheimer, Julius 68
Oppenheimer, Katherine 71
Oppenheimer, Peter 71
optically active crystals 3. *See also* crystals
orthopedic surgery 50
oscillators 103
ovary *119*, 120
oviduct *119*
ovulation 120
ozone layer xviii

## P
paleobiology xix
pancreas 52–54
particles, subatomic 19, 29
Pasteur, Jean-Joseph 2
Pasteur, Jeanne 2
Pasteur, Louis xix, *1*, 1–17
Pasteur Institute 15, 27
pasteurization 9
Pauli's exclusion principle 74
pébrine 9
pesticide xix, 91–95, *92*, *94*
phosphorous 29
piezoelectricity 22
pioneers xx
pitchblende 23
plasmid 58, 137
plutonium 76
Poland 20
Polge, E. J. Chris 145
polonium 19, 23, 27, 29
polymerase chain reaction xix, 135–140, *136*
positron 71
potassium uranyl sulfate 22
Preece, William 40
pregnancy. *See* ectopic pregnancy; in vitro fertilization
profit xvii
progesterone 122
proteins 52
protons 36, 71, 74

## Q
quantum mechanics 69
quiescence 149

## R
rabies 13–14
racemic acid 3–4, *5*
racism, of William Shockley 110
radar 45
radiation poisoning 24, 25–27
radiation therapy 25–26
radio xix, 36–43, *39*, *44*, 103
radioactive transformation 28–29
radioactivity 19–20, 22–24
radium 19, 23, 25–26, 27, 28
radium chloride 25
Radium Institute 27
radium isolation *24*
receiver 38
restriction enzyme 133
Richards, Ellen Swallow 85
Righi, Augusto 35, 36, 37
Robertson, Marion 61
Röntgen, Wilhelm 22
Roux, Émile 12
Russia 20
Rutherford, Ernest 28, 69

## S
salt 3
satellites 33
Schrieffer, John Robert 105
science xi. *See also* STS (science, technology, and society)

*Science and the Common Understanding* (Oppenheimer) 80
scientific method xi–xii
*Sea Around Us, The* (Carson) 90
*Second Creation: Dolly and the Age of Biological Control, The* (Wilmut, Campbell, Tudge) 153
semen 145
semiconductors 104–106
*Sense of Wonder, The* (Carson) 91
Seton, Ernest Thompson 86
sexually transmitted disease 117
Shockley, Mary Bradford 102
Shockley, William xix, *101*, 101–112
Shockley, William Hillman 102
*Silent Spring* (Carson) xix, 86, 90, 93–95
silicon 29, 105
silicon dioxide 62
silicosis 62
silk 9–10
skin cancer xviii
skin cells 25–26
Skłodowska, Bonia 21, 30
Skłodowska, Josef 30
Skłodowska, Marya. *See* Curie, Marie
smallpox 12
Smith, Herbert 69
society xvii–xviii
sociology xviii
Soddy, Frederick 28
Solter, Davor 144
Soviet Union 79–80
spaceflight xi
Spemann, Hans 143
spontaneous generation 7
Stalin, Joseph 71

Starr, Clarence L. 50
stem cells 147, 151
Steptoe, Grace Maud Mimms 116
Steptoe, Harry Arthur 116
Steptoe, Patrick xix, *115*, 115–127
stereochemistry 4
sterilization 8–10
Stoffel, Susan 138
STS (science, technology, and society) xvii–xviii
subatomic particles 19, 29
sugar 3, 6, 52
sulfa drugs 15
sunburn xviii
superovulation 120
surgery 12
surgery, laparoscopic 117–118
swan-necked flasks 8, *8*

## T

tartaric acid 3–4, *5*
technology xvii–xviii
telegraph 34, 36–43, *39*, *44*
telephone 34
*Thermus aquaticus* 138–139
Thomson, Sir Joseph John 69
Thoreau, Henry David 85
thorium 19, 23
*Titanic*, RMS 43
transformation, radioactive 28–29
transistors 106–108, *108*, *109*, 111, *111*
transmitter 37, *39*
Truman, Harry S. 78
tuberculosis 10, 20
Tudge, Colin 153

## U

*Under the Seawind* (Carson) 88–89
Universities, Flying 21

uranium 19, 22–23. *See also* atomic weapons
urine 49, 52
uterus *119*

## V

vaccines xix, 10, 12–14
vacuum tubes 101, 103
valence 105–106
vegetative propagation 146
Victoria (queen of Great Britain) 41

## W

*Walden* (Thoreau) 85
water purification 3
wavelength 36–37, *37*
waves, electromagnetic 36–37, *37*
Willadsen, Steen 147
Williamson, Henry 86
Wilmut, David 144
Wilmut, Ian xix–xx, *143*, 143–155
Wilmut, Vivienne 145
wine 9–10
wireless communication 36–43, *44*
World War I 27
World War II 72

## X

X-rays 22, 27

## Y

yeast 6

## Z

zygote 120, 146
zygote intrafallopian transfer 124, 125

CHICAGO PUBLIC LIBRARY
CONRAD SULZER REGIONAL LIBRARY
4455 N. LINCOLN
CHICAGO, IL 60625